"A MASTERCLASS IN OBSERVABILITY"

011Y *explained*

THE OBSERVABILITY BOOK

DANIEL SALT

Title: O11Y Explained
Author: Daniel Salt

"Observability promotes both accountability and transparency, aligning everyone, from developers and operations teams to product managers and executives, around a common understanding of system behaviour."

Daniel Salt

Foreword

Observability is not just a technical concept; it's a revolution in the way we approach and understand complex systems. In "O11Y Explained," Daniel Salt provides an invaluable resource that not only demystifies this transformative discipline but also empowers readers to harness its full potential.

As the world becomes increasingly digital, organisations are faced with the ever-growing challenge of ensuring their systems are not only functional but also performant, secure, and adaptable. Observability is the key that opens the door to a new era of system management, where understanding and optimisation are not just aspirations but attainable goals.

It's profound impact that observability can have on the success of businesses, the efficiency of operations, and the satisfaction of customers. It's a concept that transcends industries and sectors, resonating with anyone responsible for managing technology.

Daniel Salt's extensive experience in the field shines through in every chapter of this book. His ability to distil complex concepts into understandable and actionable insights is a testament to his expertise. Whether you're a seasoned professional or just beginning your journey in technology, you'll find immense value in the knowledge shared within these pages.

This book is not just a theoretical exploration of observability; it's a practical guide that equips you with the tools, strategies, and best practices needed to implement observability effectively in your own environment. It's a call to action, encouraging you to embrace the observability revolution and embrace a culture of continuous improvement.

In "O11Y Explained," you'll discover how observability transcends the boundaries of monitoring, logging, and metrics to offer a holistic view of your systems. You'll learn how to create meaningful dashboards, set up alerts that matter, and leverage observability to troubleshoot issues with precision. Daniel also takes you on a journey through the intricacies of containers, microservices, performance optimisation, security, and compliance, all through the lens of observability.

But this book is more than just a technical manual; it's an invitation to become part of a community of observability champions. It's an opportunity to join the ranks of those who understand that observability is not just a tool or a process—it's a mindset that can transform the way we build, manage, and evolve our systems.

An invitation for you to embark on this enlightening journey through Observability and embrace the future of technology with confidence. Daniel Salt's guidance will equip you with the knowledge and skills to not only navigate the complexities of modern software development and operations but to thrive in an ever-evolving landscape.

Contents

Chapter 1: Fundamentals of Observability
- Defining observability in the context of software systems.
- The differences between observability, monitoring, and logging.
- The history and evolution of observability in software.

Chapter 2: Observability Tools and Technologies
- Exploring popular observability tools and platforms (e.g., Prometheus, Grafana, Elasticsearch, Jaeger, OpenTelemetry).
- Comparing the strengths and weaknesses of various observability solutions.
- Providing guidance on choosing the right tools for different use cases.
- Future trends and Emergent Technologies

Chapter 3: Data Collection and Instrumentation
- Explaining the importance of data collection in observability.
- Discussing best practices for instrumenting code and applications.
- Covering techniques for collecting metrics, traces, and logs effectively.

Chapter 4: Metrics, Traces, and Logs
- Diving deeper into the three pillars of observability: metrics, traces, and logs.
- Explaining how these data types complement each other in providing insights.
- Discussing common formats and standards (e.g., OpenMetrics, OpenTracing, and structured logging).

Chapter 5: Building Observability into Microservices
- Exploring observability challenges specific to microservices architectures.
- Discussing strategies for instrumenting and monitoring microservices.
- Sharing best practices for managing distributed traces and logs.

Chapter 6: Visualisation and Dashboards
- Highlighting the importance of data visualisation in observability.
- Providing guidance on creating effective dashboards and alerts.
- Showcasing real-world examples of observability dashboards.

Chapter 7: Alerting and Anomaly Detection
- Discussing the role of alerting in observability.
- Explaining how to set up meaningful alerts based on metrics and traces.
- Introducing anomaly detection techniques and their significance.

Chapter 8: Troubleshooting and Debugging
- Strategies for using observability data to troubleshoot and debug issues.
- Step-by-step guidance for diagnosing common problems.
- Case studies and real-world examples of successful debugging.

Chapter 9: Scalability and Performance Optimisation
- How observability can help in optimising system performance.
- Strategies for scaling observability solutions as your infrastructure grows.
- Techniques for identifying and resolving performance bottlenecks.

Chapter 10: Security and Compliance
- The role of observability in security and compliance.
- Methods for monitoring security events and detecting

vulnerabilities.
- Addressing observability best practices for meeting regulatory requirements.

Chapter 11: Continuous Improvement and Culture
- The importance of a culture of observability.
- Strategies for fostering a culture of continuous improvement.
- How observability can drive DevOps and agile practices.

Chapter 12: The Future of Observability
- AI and Machine Learning
- Serverless, Edge and IOT Observability
- Standardisation and Open Source

Conclusion
Appendices and Glossary of observability-related terms.
- Additional resources for further reading and learning.

DANIEL SALT

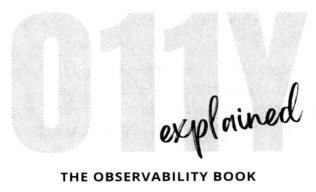

THE OBSERVABILITY BOOK

Introduction

I n the world of technology, where innovation and transformation happen at breakneck speed, a single concept has risen to prominence, transforming the way we understand, manage, and optimise complex systems: Observability.

Why Observability Matters

The performance, reliability, and security of software systems are more critical than ever. Understanding how these systems behave and having the ability to gain deep insights into their inner workings. Meaning observability—is a prerequisite for success.

Imagine having a powerful telescope that unveils the mysteries of the world around you. With this telescope, you can peer into the hidden details of complex solar systems, uncover concealed constellations and galaxies, and predict potential changes before they arise. Well, in the world of technology, there's a similar tool known as "observability."

Reading a book on observability is like looking through that powerful telescope, but instead of distant stars and galaxies, you're exploring the inner workings of intricate systems. It's your opportunity to unlock the concealed facets of the digital universe and gain profound insight into the performance, health, and efficiency of your technological systems.

Here's why you should be captivated by the idea of exploring observability: It's not limited to tech experts or IT aficionados. It's a transformative concept for anyone who interacts with the digital world. Whether you're a software developer, a business executive, or simply a curious individual navigating the digital landscape with your smartphone, observability offers the chance to understand the hidden forces that underpin our modern lives.

Observability becomes your telescope, your instrument of exploration, empowering you to:

Reveal Hidden Anomalies: Much like using a telescope to uncover obscured details, you can identify and address elusive issues within digital systems, such as slow-performing apps or tricky website glitches.

Optimise Operations: For business leaders, observability acts as your strategic tool to enhance efficiency. You can pinpoint bottlenecks, streamline processes, and optimise resource utilisation, ultimately bolstering your organisation's success.

Predict Patterns: Your digital telescope allows you to forecast when and where potential issues may emerge, offering a unique vantage point to stay ahead of looming challenges.

Enhance User Experiences: If your goal is to create digital products and services that captivate users, observability provides valuable insights into user behaviour, preferences, and pain points, enabling you to design experiences that truly engage and delight.

Pioneer Innovation: Tech moves quickly, observability knowledge places you at the forefront of innovation, much like explorers venturing into uncharted territories.

Unlock Career Avenues: Regardless of your professional level, expertise in observability is a sought-after asset in today's job market. It opens doors to exciting roles and lucrative opportunities.

So, whether you're peering through the lens of the observability telescope for the first time or seeking to deepen your understanding, this book will become your telescope to observe and decode the hidden forces of the digital world. It's your invitation to embark on an exhilarating journey, equipping you with the knowledge that can reshape your comprehension of technology and, consequently, reshape your world.

Observability transcends the boundaries of traditional monitoring and logging; it encompasses metrics, traces, and logs in a holistic ecosystem that brings clarity to the chaos of modern technology stacks. It's a journey that spans from the heart of your code to the far reaches of your infrastructure, providing invaluable insights every step of the way.

Ready to embark on this journey?

Chapter 1

Chapter 1: Fundamentals of Observability

I n the opening chapter, I will lay the foundation for our journey into the world of observability. This chapter serves as an introduction into the concept of Observability, providing essential insights into the core principles and historical context of observability in software systems.

In the context of software systems, the concept of observability has emerged as a fundamental pillar for understanding, managing, and optimising the intricate digital ecosystems that power our world. Observability equips us with the means to gain unprecedented insights into the inner workings of our software, enabling us to build, maintain, and troubleshoot with a level of clarity and precision that was once unattainable.

At its core, observability is the art and science of comprehending how a system behaves by observing its external outputs.

It's a bit like having a window into the heart of a complex machine, allowing us to witness its operations without the need for disassembly. In the context of software systems, observability provides a similar vantage point, affording us the ability to understand how our applications and infrastructure components function, perform, and interact, all while they continue to operate in real-time.

Observability as a concept is not entirely new or original. As a concept in the field of computer science and systems monitoring it also doesn't have a single creator. It has evolved over time as a response to the growing complexity of software systems and the need to understand and troubleshoot them effectively.

Observability draws from various fields, including control theory, software engineering, and operations, and it has been shaped by the contributions of many individuals and organisations. Engineers, developers, and researchers in the software and IT industry have collectively developed and refined the principles and practices associated with observability.

While there may not be a single individual responsible for creating observability, it's important to recognise that companies and thought leaders in the tech industry have played a significant role in popularising and advancing the concept. Companies like Google, IBM, Netflix, and others have contributed to the development and adoption of observability practices through their own experiences in managing complex distributed systems.

In essence, observability is the result of a collaborative effort within the technology community, with many experts and organisations working together to address the challenges of monitoring and understanding complex systems in a digital world.

For this reason, observability is far from being a single tool or a specific practice; it is a comprehensive approach that encompasses a diverse array of techniques, tools, and methodologies. Within this framework, we bring together the capture of critical metrics, the tracing of request flows, and the recording of detailed logs, constructing a wide and detailed view that empowers us to monitor the health of our systems, diagnose issues with precision, and optimise performance—all while maintaining seamless operations.

In the rest of this opening chapter, we will embark on an exploration of the fundamental concepts that underpin observability, setting the stage for an understanding of the essence of observability itself, the process of distinguishing it from related practices such as monitoring and logging, and a historical exploration of its roots, tracing its lineage from control theory to its dynamic evolution we see today, within the ever-shifting realm of software.

As we navigate through this chapter, you will hopefully find yourself equipped with a good foundation upon which to build your knowledge and skills in observability. This chapter also helps with understanding the more comprehensive exploration that awaits in the subsequent chapters of this book, each contributing to the construction of a holistic and practical understanding of observability. By the time you conclude this book, you will be primed and prepared to navigate the intricate landscape of observability with confidence and proficiency.

1.1 Defining Observability

Observability, in the context of software systems, we now know, is the ability to gain a deep understanding of how a system behaves internally without directly interfering with its operations. It's about having the tools and techniques to observe and measure various aspects of your system's performance, reliability, and security in real-time. This definition sets the stage for our exploration, emphasising the importance of insight without intrusion.

In the realm of software systems, the term "observability" has gained significant traction in recent years, but what does it truly mean, and why is it a crucial concept to grasp? In our quest to unravel the mysteries of observability, let us embark on a journey to delve deeper into the core essence of this fundamental concept. At the heart of observability lies the power to perceive, understand, and manage complex software systems—an ability that has transformed the way we approach the development and operation of digital ecosystems.

Observability is about having the tools and methodologies at our disposal to peer into the black box of a complex software system. It allows us to ask questions like: "What is happening inside the system right now?" "How are requests flowing through the system?" "What are the system's resource utilisation patterns?" These questions are pivotal in understanding and managing software systems effectively.

But this definition is only the tip of the observability iceberg. To truly grasp its essence, we must explore further.

Metrics, Traces, and Logs

One of the critical dimensions of observability is the capture and analysis of metrics, traces, and logs. These three components work in harmony to provide a comprehensive view of system behaviour.

Metrics serve as the quantitative backbone of observability. They provide numerical data about the performance, health, and behaviour of a system. Metrics can include anything from CPU usage percentages and response times to error rates and network latency. They offer a high-level overview of system performance, enabling us to identify trends, anomalies, and potential issues.

Traces, on the other hand, allow us to follow the journey of a request as it traverses a distributed system. They provide a contextual narrative of how requests move through various components, services, and microservices. Traces help us understand the dependencies and interactions within our systems, making them invaluable for troubleshooting and optimising performance.

Logs are the textual records of events, messages, and errors generated by a system. Logs offer a rich source of detailed information, often including timestamps, request IDs, and error descriptions. They are indispensable for diagnosing issues, conducting post-incident analyses, and auditing system behaviour.

When these three components—metrics, traces, and logs—are combined and analysed holistically, they create a powerful observability ecosystem. It's like having a multi-sensory experience of your software system, where metrics provide quantitative feedback, traces offer the narrative, and logs furnish the context.

Real-Time Insights

Another crucial part of observability is its emphasis on real-time insights. Observability is not about gazing into the past but about having a continuous, real-time view of your system. This real-time aspect sets it apart from traditional monitoring practices, which often involve periodic data collection and reporting.

Observability enables us to monitor and understand system behaviour in real-time. It allows us to detect anomalies as they occur, investigate issues as they unfold, and respond proactively to changes in system conditions. This real-time feedback loop is essential for maintaining the health and reliability of modern software systems, especially in dynamic and rapidly changing environments.

Beyond Reactive to Proactive

Observability is not merely a reactive tool for troubleshooting; it is also a proactive strategy for system optimisation and improvement. With observability in place, we can detect potential issues and bottlenecks before they escalate into critical problems. We can identify performance bottlenecks, optimise resource utilisation, and ensure that our systems meet their service level objectives (SLOs) consistently.

The proactive aspect of observability aligns with a broader industry trend—the shift from reactive incident management to proactive incident prevention. By continuously monitoring and analysing system behaviour, observability allows us to anticipate and mitigate issues, reducing downtime and enhancing user experiences.

Cultural Implications

Beyond its technical dimensions, observability also has cultural implications. It fosters a culture of transparency, collaboration, and shared responsibility within organisations. Teams that embrace observability are more likely to collaborate effectively, break down silos, and work towards common goals—ensuring the reliability and performance of their systems.

This cultural shift is vital, particularly in the context of modern software development, which often involves distributed teams working on complex systems. Observability aligns everyone, from developers and operations teams to product managers and executives, around a common understanding of system behaviour.

The Unifying Thread

In summary, observability is a multifaceted concept with several key dimensions:

1. The Capacity for Insights: Observability allows us to gain insights into system behaviour without disrupting operations.

2. Metrics, Traces, and Logs: It encompasses the capture and analysis of metrics, traces, and logs, providing a holistic view of system behaviour.

3. Real-Time Insights: Observability emphasises real-time monitoring and understanding of system behaviour.

4. Proactive Optimisation: It enables proactive issue detection, performance optimisation, and incident prevention.

5. Cultural Implications: Observability fosters a culture of transparency, collaboration, and shared responsibility within organisations.

These dimensions together form the unifying thread of observability. As we venture further into this book, we will explore each of these dimensions in greater detail, equipping you with the knowledge and tools necessary to embrace observability fully. Observability is not just a concept; it's a transformative methodology that can help you to reshape the way you build, operate, and optimise your software systems.

Observability in the Context of AIOps

Before we conclude this section, it's essential to touch on the relationship between observability and AIOps (Artificial Intelligence for IT Operations). AIOps is a field I personally work in, that leverages artificial intelligence and machine learning to enhance IT operations, including monitoring, event management, and incident resolution.

Observability and AIOps should be intricately connected. Observability provides the rich data and context that AIOps systems require to operate effectively. By feeding accurate observability data into AI and machine learning models, organisations can automate extremely efficient issue detection, root cause analysis, and incident resolution. This synergy between observability and AIOps represents the cutting edge of IT operations, where human expertise and machine intelligence collaborate to ensure the reliability and performance of digital systems.

As we progress through this book, we will explore the intersection of observability and AIOps in greater detail, highlighting how these two disciplines complement each other and drive innovation in the field of IT operations.

With this understanding of the fundamentals of observability, we have laid a solid foundation for our journey through the world of software systems observability. But before I move on I want us to delve a little deeper into each dimension of observability, exploring metrics, traces, logs, real-time insights, proactive optimisation, and the cultural shifts that observability fosters. Together, these facets will empower you to harness the full potential of observability in your quest to build and manage reliable, high-performance software systems.

1.2 Observability Vs. Monitoring Vs. Logging

To build a solid foundation, we need first to distinguish between observability, monitoring, and logging—three closely related concepts that are often used interchangeably but serve distinct purposes. Observability is the overarching principle that encompasses both monitoring and logging. Monitoring primarily focuses on capturing high-level system metrics, while logging delves into recording detailed events and messages. Understanding these differences is crucial to harnessing the full potential of observability.

Observability is the comprehensive practice of understanding how a system behaves by examining its external outputs —metrics, traces, and logs—without interfering with its operations. It provides a holistic view of system health and performance in real-time. Observability is proactive, emphasising early issue detection and prevention. It goes beyond reactive problem-solving, enabling organisations to optimise their systems continuously.

Key Characteristics of Observability

- Real-time Insights: Observability offers a real-time view of system behaviour, allowing for immediate issue detection and

response.
- Comprehensive Data: It combines metrics, traces, and logs to provide a complete picture of system operations.
- Proactive: Observability empowers organisations to anticipate and prevent issues, improving system reliability and performance.

Monitoring

Monitoring focuses on collecting and analysing data—usually in the form of metrics—about a system's performance and health. Monitoring tools provide a high-level overview of system conditions and are typically used to set thresholds and trigger alerts when predefined conditions are met or violated.

Key Characteristics of Monitoring

- Threshold-Based Alerts: Monitoring tools use predefined thresholds to trigger alerts when conditions exceed or fall below expected limits.
- Historical Data: Monitoring provides historical data, enabling organisations to track system performance over time.
- Response-Oriented: Monitoring is often reactive, triggering alerts when issues arise but not necessarily providing in-depth insights into the root causes.

Logging

Logging involves the recording of events, messages, and errors generated by a system. Logs provide a textual record of what has transpired within an application or infrastructure. Logging is crucial for debugging, auditing, and post-incident analysis, as it captures detailed event information.

Key Characteristics of Logging

- Detailed Records: Logs provide detailed information, including timestamps, error messages, request IDs, and contextual data.
- Auditing and Compliance: Logs are essential for auditing,

ensuring compliance with regulations, and investigating security incidents.
- Post-Incident Analysis: Logs are valuable for analysing issues after they occur, helping to identify the root causes.

Synergy between Observability, Monitoring, and Logging

While observability, monitoring, and logging are distinct practices, they are not mutually exclusive. In fact, they complement each other to provide a comprehensive view of system behaviour.

- Observability encompasses all three: Observability integrates metrics, traces, and logs to create a holistic view of system operations. It offers real-time insights while also leveraging historical data.

- Monitoring serves as an early warning system: Monitoring tools play a crucial role in alerting organisations to potential issues. When predefined thresholds are crossed, alerts are triggered, prompting further investigation through observability.

- Logging provides context: Logs offer detailed event records that provide essential context for understanding issues and incidents detected through monitoring and observability. They enable post-incident analysis and auditing.

In summary, observability, monitoring, and logging are distinct yet interconnected practices in the realm of software systems management. While each has its unique focus and purpose, they work together synergistically to ensure the reliability, performance, and security of digital ecosystems.

1.3 The Roots of Observability in Software

To understand the concept of observability fully, we must trace its origins in both control theory and the evolving landscape of software systems. Observability has a rich history, and its adaptation to the world of software is a testament to its enduring relevance.

Control Theory

The term "observability" finds its roots in control theory, a field of engineering and mathematics. In control theory, observability refers to the property of a system that allows its internal states to be inferred from knowledge of its external outputs. It's similar to deducing the inner workings of a complex machine by observing its external behaviour.

Control theory uses observability as a fundamental concept to design and control systems effectively. The idea is that if you can observe a system's outputs and infer its internal states, you can make informed decisions to control and optimise that system.

Evolution in the World of Software

Perhaps like me you remember life before the personal computer and mobile phones. Perhaps you remember the squeal and woosh sounds of the early dial-up modems we had in our homes in the 90's. Just like the Internet. Observability made its way into the world of software as systems grew in complexity. In the early days of computing, software systems were relatively simple and often run on single machines (Monolithic). Observing and understanding their behaviour was straightforward.

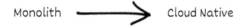

Monolith   ⟶   Cloud Native

However, as software systems evolved, they became distributed, interconnected, and highly dynamic. The rise of microservices architectures, containerisation, cloud-native technologies, and the internet itself brought about a new era of complexity. (Don't worry if these terms are new to you right now, we will cover them in more detail later).

Traditional monitoring and logging practices were ill-equipped to handle these new challenges. They provided partial visibility but lacked the depth and real-time insights required to manage modern software systems effectively.

Observability, as we know it today, emerged as a response to these challenges. It expanded the toolkit of software engineers and operators, offering a comprehensive view of system behaviour in real-time. By combining metrics, traces, and logs, observability empowered organisations to navigate the intricacies of distributed systems, container orchestration platforms, and serverless computing environments.

The Enduring Relevance of Observability

In the modern landscape of software systems, observability has become essential. It's no longer a mere option but a necessity for ensuring the reliability, performance, and security of digital ecosystems. Observability equips organisations with the means to gain deep insights, detect issues proactively, and optimise system performance continually.

As we progress through this book, we will explore how to implement observability effectively within your software systems, leverage observability tools, and cultivate a culture of continuous improvement. By the end of this journey, you'll not only understand observability in theory but be well-prepared to apply it in practice, transforming the way you build, manage, and optimise your software systems.

Chapter 2

Observability Tools and Technologies

I n Chapter 2, we dive into the dynamic world of observability tools and technologies. This chapter serves as a comprehensive guide to the diverse array of tools and platforms available to help you achieve observability excellence in your software systems.

Navigating

2.1 Navigating the Observability Landscape

Achieving a suitable level of observability has become a concern for organisations of all sizes. The ability to gain deep insights into the performance, health, and behaviour of your software applications and infrastructure is crucial for maintaining high levels of reliability and efficiency. To embark on this journey towards observability, one must navigate a diverse and rapidly expanding landscape of tools and technologies. In this section, we will explore this observability landscape, highlighting key options available to empower you in your quest for operational excellence.

Open-Source Powerhouses

Open-source observability tools have gained immense popularity owing to their flexibility, community support, and cost-effectiveness. Two standout names in this category are Prometheus and Grafana.

Prometheus is a leading open-source monitoring and alerting toolkit. It excels in collecting time-series data from various sources, enabling real-time monitoring and alerting. Prometheus boasts a powerful querying language, PromQL, which empowers users to perform complex queries to gain deep insights into system performance. Its support for multi-dimensional data and dynamic service discovery makes it a favourite among DevOps teams.

Grafana complements Prometheus by providing an intuitive and visually appealing platform for data visualisation and dashboards. It supports numerous data sources, including Prometheus, Elasticsearch, and InfluxDB, making it a versatile choice for aggregating and presenting observability data. Grafana's extensive library of plugins and a vibrant user community contribute to its popularity.

Advanced Solutions

For organisations with complex, large-scale systems and a need for advanced features, enterprise-grade observability platforms like IBM Instana and Dynatrace are often the go-to choice. However there are also two notable open source options in this category which are Elasticsearch and Jaeger.

Elasticsearch

Elasticsearch, part of the Elastic Stack (formerly known as the ELK Stack), is a powerful and versatile platform for log and event data analysis. It excels in indexing and searching vast amounts of structured and unstructured data. Elasticsearch's capabilities extend beyond simple observability, as it can also be used for log management, security information and event management (SIEM), and full-text search. Its integration with Kibana, another component of the Elastic Stack, allows for the creation of rich, customisable dashboards.

Jaeger

Distributed tracing is a vital component of observability, and Jaeger is a leading open-source solution for this purpose. It helps organisations trace requests as they flow through complex microservices architectures. By visualising the path of requests and identifying bottlenecks or issues, Jaeger aids in troubleshooting and optimising system performance. Its support for multiple programming languages and cloud-native environments makes it a valuable asset in the world of observability.

Example Use Cases

Each observability tool and technology mentioned above has its unique strengths and best use cases. The choice of tools should align with your specific organisational needs and goals:

- Use Prometheus and Grafana for real-time monitoring and alerting in dynamic environments where flexibility and customisation are key.

- Employ Elasticsearch for comprehensive log analysis and event management, particularly in security-sensitive scenarios.

- Turn to Jaeger for distributed tracing in microservices architectures, enabling efficient troubleshooting and optimisation.

Observability & APM Solutions

While open-source tools have their merits, Enterprise

organisations often require more comprehensive solutions with advanced features, support, and scalability. Observability APM (Application Performance Monitoring) solutions like IBM Instana or Dynatrace etc. cater to such needs.

Using a dedicated Observability APM platform that specialises in automated application performance monitoring. It offers real-time monitoring of applications and microservices, automatically discovering and mapping your application's architecture. Instana provides deep insights into application performance and detects anomalies out-of-the-box, making it easier to identify and resolve issues promptly. Its automatic tracing and distributed tracing capabilities help track transactions across even the most complex microservices environments.

The observability landscape offers a plethora of tools and technologies to suit the diverse needs of modern software systems. By understanding the strengths and weaknesses of each option, organisations can make informed decisions on how to achieve observability excellence in their unique contexts. The journey to operational excellence begins with the right tools.

2.2 Choosing the Right Tools

Selecting the right tools is a pivotal decision. The observability landscape, as we've explored in the previous section, offers a plethora of options, each with its unique strengths and focus areas. In this section, I will aim to provide guidance for you on how to make informed choices based on your specific needs. Whether you are primarily concerned with infrastructure monitoring, application performance management, or end-to-end tracing, my goal is to empower you to build a tailored observability stack that aligns seamlessly with your organisation's goals and constraints.

Define Your Objectives and Priorities

Start by clearly defining your observability objectives. Are you primarily interested in monitoring the health of your infrastructure, ensuring the optimal performance of your applications, or tracing end-to-end transactions? Understanding your priorities will help you narrow down your tool choices.

Assess Your Current Environment

Take a close look at your existing infrastructure, technology stack, and software architecture. Are you running a monolithic application or a microservices-based system? Do you rely on cloud services, containers, or traditional servers? Understanding your current environment is crucial for selecting tools that seamlessly integrate with your setup.

Consider Scalability and Growth

Think about the scalability of your observability solution. Will it be able to handle your growing infrastructure and user base? Scalability is especially critical for fast-growing organisations. Ensure that the tools you choose can grow with you without a significant overhaul.

Evaluate Ease of Implementation

Consider the ease of implementation and the learning curve associated with the tools. Some solutions require extensive configuration and customisation, while others offer a more straightforward setup process. Assess your team's expertise and available resources to ensure a smooth adoption process.

Budget and Cost Considerations

Budget constraints are a reality for most organisations. While open-source solutions like Prometheus and Grafana are cost-effective, paid solutions like IBM Instana or New Relic and others offer advanced features but come with licensing costs. Balance your requirements with your budget to find the right fit.

Interoperability and Ecosystem

Consider how well the tools you select integrate with your existing tech stack. Tools that offer broad compatibility and have an extensive ecosystem of plugins and integrations can save you time and effort in the long run.

Tool Performance

Assess the tools' performance in handling the volume of data generated by your systems. Make sure they can provide real-time insights and scale as your organisation grows. Performance bottlenecks can hinder the effectiveness of your observability stack.

Support and Maintenance

Evaluate the level of support and maintenance required for your chosen tools. Open-source solutions often rely on community support, while enterprise-grade options come with dedicated support teams. Factor in your organisation's ability to handle maintenance tasks and the criticality of your observability infrastructure.

Security and Compliance

Ensure that the tools you select adhere to security best practices and comply with any regulatory requirements applicable to your industry. Data security and privacy are paramount, especially when dealing with sensitive information.

Trial and Testing

Before committing to a particular tool or set of tools, conduct thorough trials and testing. Most observability solutions offer free trials or community editions that allow you to evaluate their suitability in a real-world context.

The process of choosing the right observability tools is a strategic endeavour that requires a deep understanding of your organisation's goals, infrastructure, and constraints. By defining your objectives, considering your current environment, and evaluating factors such as scalability, budget, interoperability, and support, you can make informed decisions that pave the way for a tailored observability stack. The goal is to empower your organisation with the insights and capabilities needed to achieve operational excellence in today's complex software ecosystems.

2.3 OpenTelemetry and Standardisation

In my experience as organisations grow, standardisation is crucial. I introduce you to OpenTelemetry, a powerful initiative aimed at creating open standards for instrumenting and observing applications. By understanding OpenTelemetry and its significance, you'll be better equipped to embrace and contribute to the growing observability ecosystem.

OpenTelemetry and Standardisation in Observability

In the world of software development and system operations, observability plays a pivotal role in ensuring the reliability, performance, and security of modern applications. To achieve comprehensive observability, standardisation is crucial, as it allows for seamless interoperability between various tools and systems. In this discussion, I will introduce you to OpenTelemetry, a powerful initiative aimed at creating open standards for instrumenting and observing applications. By understanding OpenTelemetry and its significance, you'll be better equipped to embrace and contribute to the growing observability ecosystem.

The Need for Standardisation in Observability

As software systems have become increasingly complex and

distributed, the need for effective observability tools and practices has grown exponentially. Observability encompasses the ability to gain insights into the inner workings of software applications and infrastructure, including monitoring, tracing, and logging. These insights are essential for diagnosing and resolving issues, optimising performance, and ensuring the overall health of systems.

However, the observability landscape is vast and fragmented, with a multitude of tools and technologies each using its own data formats and protocols. This lack of standardisation can lead to several challenges:

Interoperability Issues: Different tools often have difficulty sharing data or working together seamlessly. This can hinder the ability to create a unified view of system health.

Vendor Lock-In: Organisations may find themselves locked into specific observability toolsets due to proprietary formats and protocols, limiting their flexibility and choices.

Learning Curve: Teams must invest time in learning the specifics of each tool, which can be inefficient and counterproductive.

Data Overhead: Duplicative or inconsistent data collection can lead to increased data storage costs and unnecessary network overhead.

To address these challenges and foster a more cohesive observability ecosystem, OpenTelemetry was conceived.

Introducing OpenTelemetry

OpenTelemetry is an open-source project under the Cloud Native Computing Foundation (CNCF) that aims to provide a set of APIs, libraries, agents, and instrumentation to enable observability in software systems. The project's mission is to create open standards for observability and instrumentation, making it easier for developers and operators to collect, process, and export telemetry data from their applications.

OpenTelemetry has two primary components:

1. <u>OpenTelemetry API</u>: This defines a set of standard APIs for instrumenting code in various programming languages. These APIs provide a consistent way to capture telemetry data, including traces, metrics, and logs.

2. <u>OpenTelemetry SDK</u>: The SDK is responsible for implementing the APIs and providing instrumentation libraries for different languages and frameworks. It also includes components for collecting, processing, and exporting telemetry data to backend systems.

Key Features and Significance of OpenTelemetry

OpenTelemetry offers several key features and benefits that contribute to its significance in the observability landscape:

Vendor-Neutral: OpenTelemetry is designed to be vendor-neutral, ensuring that telemetry data can be collected and used with a wide range of observability tools and platforms.

Cross-Language Support: OpenTelemetry provides support for multiple programming languages, including Java, Python, Go, and more, making it accessible to a diverse developer community.

Unified Observability: By standardising the instrumentation of applications, OpenTelemetry helps create a unified view of observability data, simplifying the troubleshooting and optimisation process.

Community-Driven: OpenTelemetry is driven by a vibrant and collaborative community of developers, ensuring that it evolves to meet the needs of modern software systems.

Flexibility: OpenTelemetry allows users to choose their preferred backends for data processing and storage, providing flexibility and choice in observability tooling.

Interoperability: The adoption of open standards by multiple observability vendors and projects, such as Prometheus, Jaeger, and Grafana, ensures interoperability between tools that support OpenTelemetry.

Interoperability of Agents: OTLP and Vendor Agents

Observability in modern software systems relies heavily on the ability to collect, transmit, and analyse telemetry data effectively. Achieving this requires a high degree of interoperability between various components of the observability stack, including agents and vendors' proprietary agents. In this discussion, we'll explore the concept of interoperability, focusing on the OpenTelemetry Protocol (OTLP) and its role in facilitating interoperability between agents and vendor-specific agents in observability.

Understanding Interoperability

Interoperability, in the context of observability, refers to the ability of different components, tools, or systems to work together seamlessly, exchange data, and function cohesively within an observability ecosystem. In essence, it ensures that data collected by one component can be understood and processed by another, regardless of vendor or technology stack.

The Role of OTLP

The OpenTelemetry Protocol (OTLP) is an initiative in the observability landscape aimed at addressing the challenges of interoperability. OTLP provides a standardised and vendor-agnostic protocol for transmitting telemetry data, including traces, metrics, and logs. Its primary goals include:

Standardisation: OTLP standardises the format and structure of observability data, making it consistent across different observability components and tools.

Vendor Neutrality: OTLP is designed to be vendor-neutral, ensuring that telemetry data can be collected and used with a wide range of observability tools and platforms.

Cross-Language Support: OTLP offers support for multiple programming languages, enabling developers to integrate it into their applications regardless of the tech stack used.

Community-Driven: OTLP is an open-source project that encourages community collaboration and contributions, further enhancing its flexibility and adaptability.

Vendor-Specific Agents

Many observability vendors offer their own agents, which are software components responsible for collecting telemetry data from applications and sending it to their respective observability platforms. These vendor-specific agents are often optimised for their particular observability stack and may offer unique features.

While vendor-specific agents provide deep integration and specialised capabilities, they can sometimes lead to vendor lock-in, making it challenging to switch observability platforms or tools. This is where OTLP plays a crucial role in ensuring interoperability.

Interoperability with OTLP

To achieve interoperability between vendor-specific agents and the wider observability ecosystem, these agents can be designed to support the OTLP protocol. This means that, in addition to sending telemetry data to their proprietary observability platforms, these agents can also send data in the standardised OTLP format to be consumed by other tools and platforms that support OTLP.

Interoperability with OTLP offers several benefits:

Flexibility: Organisations can use vendor-specific agents for their unique features and still maintain the ability to integrate with other observability tools that support OTLP.

Vendor Neutrality: Data collected by vendor-specific agents can be used with observability tools from different vendors, reducing vendor lock-in concerns.

Unified Observability: By embracing OTLP, organisations can create a unified view of observability data, making it easier to troubleshoot and optimise performance across their entire stack.

The Future of Interoperability

As observability continues to evolve, interoperability will remain a critical consideration. The adoption of standardised protocols like OTLP is expected to grow, further enhancing the interoperability of observability components. Additionally, organisations and vendors are likely to continue embracing open standards to ensure that telemetry data can flow seamlessly between different parts of the observability stack.

Interoperability is essential for building effective observability ecosystems that can adapt to the dynamic nature of modern software systems. OTLP, as a standardised and vendor-agnostic protocol, plays a pivotal role in achieving this interoperability by allowing vendor-specific agents to communicate with other tools and platforms in a consistent and standardised manner. Embracing interoperability through initiatives like OTLP ensures that organisations have the flexibility and choice to use the observability tools that best suit their needs while maintaining the ability to integrate with a wide range of observability components.

Getting Started with OpenTelemetry

To get started with OpenTelemetry, you can follow these key

steps:

1. Instrumentation: Developers can use OpenTelemetry APIs and instrumentation libraries to add telemetry collection to their applications. This involves capturing data on traces (request/response chains), metrics (performance metrics), and logs.

2. Backend Configuration: Choose a backend system for telemetry data collection and storage. OpenTelemetry supports various backends, including cloud-based observability platforms and on-premises solutions (like IBM Instana).

3. Exporter Configuration: Configure exporters to send telemetry data to the chosen backend. This can involve setting up connections and specifying formats.

4. Integration with Existing Tools: Integrate OpenTelemetry with existing observability tools, dashboards, and visualisation platforms to gain insights into the performance and health of your systems.

5. Community Engagement: Participate in the OpenTelemetry community by contributing to the project, reporting issues, or sharing best practices with other users.

"...embracing OpenTelemetry can be an important strategic decision for organisations seeking to harness the full potential of observability data."

OpenTelemetry is a powerful initiative that addresses the critical need for standardisation in the observability landscape. By providing open standards for instrumenting and observing applications, OpenTelemetry empowers organisations to create unified and interoperable observability ecosystems. This, in turn, enhances the ability to diagnose issues, optimise performance, and maintain the health of software systems.

In my opinion, as the observability ecosystem continues to evolve, embracing OpenTelemetry can be an important strategic decision for organisations seeking to harness the full potential of observability data. It offers a path towards greater flexibility, interoperability, and collaboration in the ever-evolving world of software development and operations.

By adopting OpenTelemetry, organisations can take significant steps toward achieving observability excellence and ensuring the reliability and performance of their modern applications.

2.4 Future Trends and Emerging Technologies

Observability is a field in constant evolution. I provide a glimpse into emerging technologies and trends, such as distributed tracing, AI-driven observability, and serverless observability. These insights offer a glimpse into the future of observability and help you stay ahead in a rapidly changing landscape.

Future Trends and Emerging Technologies in Observability

The field of observability is in a constant state of evolution, driven by the ever-increasing complexity of modern software systems and the demand for deeper insights into their behaviour. Staying ahead in this rapidly changing landscape requires a keen eye on emerging technologies and trends that shape the future of observability. In this discussion, we'll explore some of these exciting developments, including distributed tracing, AI-driven observability, and serverless observability.

Distributed Tracing

As microservices architectures and containerisation become

mainstream, distributed tracing has gained prominence as a critical observability tool. Distributed tracing allows organisations to track the flow of requests across multiple services, providing end-to-end visibility into application performance. In the future, we can expect the following trends:

Standardisation: Efforts like OpenTelemetry are driving the standardisation of distributed tracing, making it easier for organisations to adopt and integrate tracing into their observability stacks.

Advanced Analytics: Distributed tracing data will be used for more sophisticated analytics, enabling organisations to identify performance bottlenecks, optimise resource allocation, and enhance the user experience.

Distributed Context Propagation: Technologies like context propagation frameworks will become more prevalent, ensuring that trace context seamlessly carries across service boundaries, even in highly distributed environments.

AI-Driven Observability

Artificial intelligence (AI) and machine learning (ML) are set to revolutionise observability by automating analysis and anomaly detection. The future of AI-driven observability includes:

Anomaly Detection: AI algorithms will become adept at identifying abnormal behaviour within observability data, allowing for proactive issue resolution and predictive maintenance.

Root Cause Analysis: Machine learning models will assist in pinpointing the root causes of performance issues, reducing mean time to resolution (MTTR) significantly.

Automated Remediation: AI-driven systems will not only detect issues but also automate remediation actions, minimising human intervention in the observability loop.

Serverless Observability

The rise of serverless computing has introduced unique challenges for observability, given the ephemeral and event-driven nature of serverless functions. Future trends in serverless observability include:

Specialised Tools: We can expect the development of specialised observability tools tailored to the nuances of serverless architectures, such as AWS Lambda or Azure Functions.

Deeper Insights: Enhanced observability solutions will provide deeper insights into the performance of individual functions, helping organisations optimise resource allocation and reduce latency.

Event-Driven Tracing: Observability solutions will support event-driven tracing, allowing organisations to trace the execution path of events as they move through serverless functions.

Observability as Code

Observability as Code (OAC) is an emerging trend where observability configurations are managed and versioned alongside application code. This approach offers several benefits:

Infrastructure as Code Integration: OAC integrates observability settings into infrastructure as code (IaC) pipelines, ensuring consistency and reproducibility.

Scalability and Agility: By treating observability as code, organisations can scale observability configurations as applications grow, promoting agility and reducing manual overhead.

Collaboration: Developers and operations teams can collaborate more effectively by versioning and sharing observability configurations through code repositories.

Quantum Observability

As quantum computing technologies continue to advance, observability in the quantum realm becomes a unique challenge. Future trends in quantum observability may include:

Quantum Tracing: Tools and methodologies for tracing the behaviour of quantum algorithms and qubits to identify and debug issues.

Quantum Security Observability: Monitoring quantum cryptographic systems to ensure the security and integrity of quantum communications.

Quantum Instrumentation: Developing observability tools that can interface with and monitor quantum hardware for research and development purposes.

Observability is a fascinating field that is constantly adapting to the evolving landscape of software architecture and technology. Emerging trends such as distributed tracing, AI-driven observability, serverless observability, Observability as Code, and even quantum observability are shaping the future of how we gain insights into the behaviour and performance of complex systems. Staying informed about these trends and embracing relevant technologies will be essential for organisations striving to maintain operational excellence in the ever-changing world of software and technology. It's also a likely reason as to why you are reading this book.

Ok, so hopefully you now have an improved understanding of the observability tools and technologies available to you. You'll be prepared to make informed decisions when building or enhancing your observability stack, ensuring that you have the right tools to gain the insights you need into your software systems. This knowledge sets the stage for our deep dive into observability practices in the subsequent chapters of the book.

Chapter 3

Data Collection and Instrumentation

C hapter 3, delves into the critical processes of data collection and instrumentation, which are fundamental to achieving a high level of observability in software systems.

Collecting Data

3.1 The Essence of Data Collection

This chapter begins by emphasising the fundamental importance of data collection in the observability landscape. It highlights how data collection is the lifeblood of observability, providing the raw materials necessary for insights and analysis. Whether you're tracking metrics, tracing requests, or logging events, effective data collection is the cornerstone of your observability efforts.

3.1 The Foundation Of Observability: Data Collection

Observability, at its core, is about gaining insights into the inner workings of software applications and infrastructure. It encompasses monitoring system health, tracing the flow of requests, and logging critical events. Yet, all these facets of observability share a common foundation: the collection of data.

Data collection serves as the cornerstone upon which observability is built. It is the process of gathering information, metrics, traces, and logs from various components of a software system. This data, when effectively collected and structured, forms the basis for understanding system behaviour, diagnosing issues, and optimising performance.

The Nature of Data Collection

Data collection in observability is a multifaceted endeavour, encompassing various types of data:

Metrics: Metrics provide quantitative measurements of system attributes and performance. They can include CPU usage, memory consumption, response times, and error rates. Collecting metrics helps track the overall health of a system and identifies trends and anomalies.

Traces: Tracing is concerned with the journey of a request as it traverses through different components of a distributed system. Distributed tracing enables the visualisation of request paths and aids in identifying bottlenecks, latency issues, and dependencies.

Logs: Logs capture events, activities, and system messages generated during the execution of an application or infrastructure. Log data is invaluable for troubleshooting, auditing, and understanding the context of specific events.

The Significance of Effective Data Collection:

Effective data collection in observability serves several critical purposes:

Issue Detection: By continuously collecting data, observability tools can quickly detect and alert you to anomalies, errors, or performance degradations, enabling timely issue resolution.

Performance Optimisation: Data collection allows you to identify performance bottlenecks, resource constraints, and areas where optimisation efforts are needed. Metrics and traces provide insights into where improvements can be made.

Root Cause Analysis: In the event of an incident or system failure, collected data plays a crucial role in root cause analysis. Traces and logs help trace the sequence of events that led to the issue.

Capacity Planning: By tracking resource utilisation over time, collected metrics assist in capacity planning, ensuring that infrastructure can handle anticipated loads.

Challenges and Considerations in Data Collection

While data collection is foundational to observability, it is not without challenges:

Data Volume: Collecting large volumes of data can be overwhelming and costly. Effective sampling and filtering mechanisms are essential to manage data volume.

Data Quality: Inaccurate or inconsistent data can lead to incorrect conclusions. Ensuring data quality through validation and error handling is crucial.

Privacy and Security: Collecting sensitive data must be done in compliance with privacy regulations and security best practices. Anonymisation and encryption may be necessary.

Instrumentation: Proper instrumentation of code and infrastructure is essential for data collection. It requires careful planning and integration with observability tools.

The Data-Driven Future of Observability

Data collection stands as the lifeblood of observability in software systems. It empowers organisations to gain insights, optimise performance, and ensure system reliability. The data-driven future of observability promises a deeper understanding of software behaviour, faster issue resolution, and a proactive approach to system management.

As we continue our exploration of data collection and instrumentation in this chapter, it becomes evident that they are not just processes; they are the essence of observability itself, enabling organisations to navigate the complex and dynamic world of modern software systems with confidence and precision.

3.2 Instrumenting Your Code and Applications

In this section we will explore the practical aspects of instrumenting your code and applications. You'll learn how to embed observability hooks and gather essential data points from within your software. We cover best practices for selecting and implementing instrumentation libraries, ensuring that you can capture the right data without introducing undue complexity.

Instrumenting

Instrumentation for Observability: A Simplified Explanation with Code Examples

Instrumentation is a vital process in the world of software observability. It involves adding specific code snippets to your applications to collect data and gain insights into their behaviour. In this simplified explanation, we'll explore what instrumentation is and provide code examples in Python to illustrate the concept.

What Is Instrumentation?

Instrumentation, in the context of software observability, is like adding sensors to a complex machine to understand how it's functioning. It's about collecting data from your software, such as metrics (performance measurements) and traces (request flow), so you can monitor, diagnose, and optimise your applications effectively.

Why Is Instrumentation Important?

Instrumentation is crucial because it provides you with the necessary data to:

- Monitor the health of your software systems.
- Detect and resolve issues quickly.
- Optimise performance.
- Understand how your applications are used.

Now, let's dive into some simple Python examples to see how instrumentation works:

Instrumentation for Metrics

Imagine you have a Python application that handles HTTP requests, and you want to count how many requests it processes. You can do this using instrumentation for metrics.

Here's a simplified Python code snippet:

```python
import time
from opentelemetry import metrics
from             opentelemetry.exporter.prometheus        import
PrometheusMetricsExporter
from opentelemetry.sdk.metrics import MeterProvider
from             opentelemetry.sdk.metrics.export        import
MetricsExportResult

   Create a meter provider
meter_provider    MeterProvider()
metrics.set_meter_provider(meter_provider)


   Create a metrics exporter (Prometheus in this case)
exporter    PrometheusMetricsExporter()
metrics.get_meter_provider().start_pipeline(exporter)

   Create a meter
meter    meter_provider.get_meter(__name__)

   Define a counter metric
requests_counter    meter.create_counter(
   name "requests",
   description "Count of HTTP requests",
   unit "1",
   value_type int,
)

   Simulate an HTTP request
def handle_request():
   with requests_counter.bind() as bound_counter:
      bound_counter.add(1)
         Your request handling logic here
      time.sleep(0.1)     Simulating work

   Perform some requests
for _ in range(10):
   handle_request()

   Export metrics (e.g., to Prometheus)
export_result
exporter.export(meter_provider.get_interval_metric_reader())
if export_result    MetricsExportResult.SUCCESS:
   print("Metrics exported successfully")
else:
```

```
  print("Metrics export failed")
```

In this example:

- We imported the necessary OpenTelemetry libraries for metrics.
- We created a counter metric called `requests` to count HTTP requests.
- Inside the `handle_request` function, we incremented the `requests` metric by 1 for each request.
- Finally, we exported the collected metrics (e.g., to Prometheus) for further analysis.

Instrumentation for Distributed Tracing

Now, let's consider a scenario where you want to trace the flow of requests through your Python application to understand how they travel between different components. This can be achieved through instrumentation for distributed tracing.

Here's a simplified Python code snippet:

```python
import time
from opentelemetry import trace
from opentelemetry.sdk.trace import TracerProvider
from        opentelemetry.exporter.jaeger.thrift        import
JaegerExporter
from opentelemetry.sdk.trace.export import SpanExportResult

  Create a tracer provider
tracer_provider    TracerProvider()
trace.set_tracer_provider(tracer_provider)

  Create a Jaeger exporter (replace with your Jaeger agent's
host and port)
jaeger_exporter    JaegerExporter(
  agent_host_name "localhost",
  agent_port 6831,
)

  Add the exporter to the tracer provider
tracer_provider.add_span_processor(SimpleExportSpanProcessor(
```

```
jaeger_exporter))
  Create a tracer
tracer   trace.get_tracer(__name__)
  Define a function to simulate distributed work
def perform_distributed_work():
  with tracer.start_as_current_span("distributed work"):
      Simulate distributed work
    time.sleep(0.2)
  Simulate a distributed operation
perform_distributed_work()
  Export traces (e.g., to Jaeger)
export_result
jaeger_exporter.export_span(tracer_provider.get_span_processo
r())
if export_result    SpanExportResult.SUCCESS:
  print("Traces exported successfully")
else:
  print("Traces export failed")
```

In this example:

- We imported the necessary OpenTelemetry libraries for distributed tracing.
- We created a tracer to capture spans (segments of work) with a name "distributed-work" to represent our distributed operation.
- Inside the `perform_distributed_work` function, we simulated some distributed work.
- Finally, we exported the captured traces (e.g., to Jaeger) for further analysis.

Why Instrumentation Matters

Instrumentation is essential because it allows you to:

- Monitor the performance and health of your applications.
- Trace how requests flow through your code and between services.
- Collect data to diagnose issues quickly.
- Optimise your applications for better performance.

It's like having a dashboard in your car that shows you how fast you're going, how much fuel you have left, and whether your engine is running smoothly. Without instrumentation, you'd be driving blindfolded.

Instrumentation is the key to achieving observability in your software systems. By adding code to collect data, you can gain insights, monitor performance, and troubleshoot issues effectively. Whether it's counting requests or tracing their flow, instrumentation empowers you to understand your applications better and keep them running smoothly.

3.3 Collecting Metrics, Traces, and Logs

In observability, there are three primary types of data: metrics, traces, and logs. You will see I have explained this several times throughout this book. I have done this intentionally to help you to delve deep into each of these data types, explaining their unique characteristics and use cases.

My hope is that as you read through each chapter, you will build on the knowledge gained and move forwards to gain deeper insights. Assisting you to look further into how to collect and leverage metrics for real-time monitoring, traces for understanding the flow of requests through your system, and logs for detailed event and error tracking.

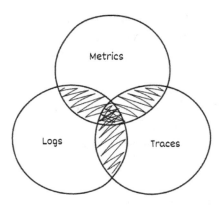

Harnessing Metrics, Traces, and Logs for Observability

In the quest for observability in software systems, collecting and harnessing data is paramount. This section explores the invaluable trio of metrics, traces, and logs, showcasing how they provide essential insights for real-time monitoring, understanding request flow, and tracking events and errors in your system. Together, these components form the foundation of effective observability.

Metrics for Real-Time Monitoring

Metrics are the heartbeat of observability, providing continuous and quantitative data about the performance and health of your software systems. They serve as real-time indicators, allowing you to monitor crucial aspects of your applications, infrastructure, and services.

Collecting Metrics

Metrics can encompass a wide range of data, including CPU usage, memory consumption, response times, and error rates. Instrumenting your code to collect metrics enables you to track these vital statistics.

Here are some examples

Metrics are quantitative measurements that provide insights into various aspects of system performance, behaviour, and resource utilisation. Here are some common examples of metrics:

CPU Usage: Measures the percentage of CPU capacity utilised by a process or system. High CPU usage may indicate resource contention or inefficiencies in code.

Memory Usage: Tracks the amount of RAM used by an application or system. Monitoring memory usage helps identify memory leaks and inefficient memory management.

Response Time: Measures the time it takes for a system or service to respond to a request. It is crucial for assessing the performance and responsiveness of applications.

Throughput: Represents the rate at which a system or service processes requests or transactions. It helps determine the system's capacity and scalability.

Error Rate: Calculates the percentage of requests or transactions that result in errors. Monitoring error rates is essential for identifying and addressing issues in applications.

Network Latency: Measures the delay in data transmission over a network. High network latency can impact application performance, especially in distributed systems.

Disk I/O: Tracks the input and output operations of a disk or storage device. Monitoring disk I/O helps identify bottlenecks and storage-related issues.

Database Queries per Second: Counts the number of queries or transactions processed by a database in a second. It helps assess database performance and scalability.

HTTP Requests per Second: Measures the rate of incoming HTTP requests to a web server or application. RPS is vital for web server optimisation and capacity planning.

Active User Sessions: Monitors the number of active user sessions or connections to a service. It helps assess user engagement and capacity planning for user-facing applications.

System Uptime: Tracks how long a system or application has been running without interruptions. It provides insights into system stability.

Queue Length: Measures the number of items in a queue, such as a message queue or task queue. Monitoring queue length helps ensure efficient task processing.

Cache Hit Rate: Calculates the percentage of requests that are served from a cache instead of fetching data from the source. A high cache hit rate indicates effective caching.

HTTP Status Codes: Counts the distribution of HTTP status codes (e.g., 200, 404, 500) in web server responses. It helps detect and diagnose HTTP-related issues.

Garbage Collection Metrics: Tracks the frequency and duration of garbage collection events in programming languages like Java. High or frequent garbage collection can impact application performance.

API Response Time: Measures the time it takes for external API calls to complete. Monitoring API response times helps identify third-party service issues.

Resource Utilisation (e.g., Disk Space, Network Bandwidth): Monitors the usage of various system resources, such as available disk space or network bandwidth.

These are just some examples of the many metrics that we can collect to gain insights into their systems' health and performance. The choice of metrics depends on the specific goals and requirements of the application and the observability platform in use.

For instance, you might monitor the average response time of your web service. By collecting this metric, you can quickly identify performance issues and respond proactively to ensure optimal user experiences.

Leveraging Metrics:

Once collected, metrics can be visualised through dashboards and graphs, enabling you to gain immediate insights into system behaviour. Anomalies and deviations from expected patterns become evident, allowing for rapid response and issue resolution.

Traces for Understanding Request Flow:

Distributed tracing is your window into understanding how requests traverse through the various components of your distributed system. Traces provide a holistic view of request flow, highlighting dependencies, bottlenecks, and latency issues.

Here are some examples

Traces, in the context of observability, represent the journey of a request or transaction as it traverses through various components of a distributed system. They provide insights into the flow and interactions of requests, helping diagnose bottlenecks, latency issues, and dependencies. Here are some common examples of traces:

HTTP Request Traces: Trace the lifecycle of an HTTP request as it enters a web server, goes through middleware, interacts with application logic, accesses a database, and generates a response. These traces help pinpoint performance issues in web applications.

Microservices Traces: In microservices architectures, traces follow requests across different microservices, tracking how they communicate with each other. This helps in identifying delays and dependencies between services.

Database Query Traces: Trace the execution of a specific database query, including the time it takes to retrieve data, process it, and return a response. Database query traces help optimise database performance.

Message Queue Traces: Monitor the flow of messages through a message queue or message broker. Traces can reveal how messages are routed, processed, and whether any delays occur in message processing.

Container Orchestration Traces: In containerised environments like Kubernetes, traces can show how requests move between containers, pods, and nodes. This helps in understanding the behaviour of containerised applications.

User Session Traces: Follow the interactions of a user session through a web application, including login, navigation, and actions taken. User session traces provide insights into user behaviour and can be used for user experience optimisation.

Payment Processing Traces: In financial applications, traces can track the steps involved in processing a payment transaction, from authentication to settlement. This helps ensure the reliability and security of financial transactions.

IoT Device Communication Traces: For Internet of Things (IoT) applications, traces can map how data is collected from IoT devices, transmitted to the cloud, and processed. This aids in troubleshooting IoT system behaviour.

API Call Traces: Trace the flow of API calls between services, whether internal or external. API call traces reveal dependencies and latencies in service-to-service communication.

Third-Party Service Integration Traces: When integrating with third-party services or APIs, traces show the interactions and response times between your application and the external service. They help identify performance bottlenecks and reliability issues with external services.

Resource Provisioning Traces: In cloud environments, traces can track the provisioning of resources like virtual machines, containers, or serverless functions. This helps optimise resource allocation and cost management.

Authentication and Authorisation Traces: Trace the authentication and authorisation process within an application to ensure security and compliance with access control policies.

Search Query Processing Traces: For search applications, traces can follow the steps involved in processing a search query, including indexing, ranking, and retrieval of search results.

E-commerce Order Processing Traces: In e-commerce platforms, traces can capture the sequence of events from order placement to payment processing, inventory management, and shipping.

These are just a few examples of the diverse use cases for traces in observability. Traces provide a comprehensive view of how requests or transactions move through complex systems, making them invaluable for diagnosing issues, optimising performance, and ensuring the reliability of distributed applications and services.

Collecting Traces: To collect traces, instrument your code to create spans, which represent individual units of work within a request. Spans are linked together to form a trace, depicting the entire journey of a request.

For example, when a user logs in, a trace can reveal the journey from the initial HTTP request to authentication, database queries, and response rendering.

Leveraging Traces: Traces empower you to troubleshoot complex issues by visualising the path of a request and pinpointing areas where bottlenecks occur. With trace data, you can optimise performance, reduce latency, and ensure smooth interactions in your system.

Logs for Detailed Event and Error Tracking

Logs serve as a detailed record of events, activities, and messages generated during the execution of your applications and infrastructure. They are invaluable for tracking events, debugging issues, and auditing system behaviour.

Here are some examples:

Logs are textual records of events, activities, and messages generated during the execution of software applications or systems. They are essential for tracking the behaviour of applications, diagnosing issues, auditing activities, and maintaining a historical record. Here are some common examples of logs:

Application Logs: Logs generated by the application itself to record its activities, errors, and informational messages. These logs provide insights into the application's behaviour and performance.

Info Logs: Informational messages that provide details about the application's state, activities, and successful operations.

Error Logs: Records of errors, exceptions, and unexpected behaviours within the application. Error logs help in identifying and diagnosing issues.

Web Server Logs: Logs generated by web servers (e.g., Apache, Nginx, or IIS) to track incoming HTTP requests, responses, and server events.

Access Logs: Record details of incoming requests, including IP addresses, requested URLs, HTTP methods, and response status codes.

Error Logs: Capture server-related errors, such as server crashes, configuration issues, or resource allocation problems.

Database Logs: Logs generated by database management systems (DBMS) to record database operations, queries, and error messages.

Query Logs: Track database queries, their execution times, and the affected tables. Query logs are essential for database optimisation.

Transaction Logs: Maintain a history of database transactions, allowing for data recovery and rollback in case of failures.

Security Logs: Logs related to security events, including authentication and authorisation activities, intrusion detection, and access control.

Audit Logs: Record all user actions and system events for compliance and auditing purposes. This includes user logins, access attempts, and data changes.

Intrusion Detection Logs: Capture suspicious or unauthorised activities, such as failed login attempts or security breaches.

Application Server Logs: Logs generated by application servers (e.g., Tomcat, JBoss) that host web applications. These logs include deployment information, performance metrics, and application-specific messages.

Deployment Logs: Track the deployment and configuration of web applications, including version changes and updates.

Performance Logs: Record performance metrics, such as response times, request counts, and memory usage, to optimise server performance.

Network Logs: Logs that monitor network activities, including network traffic, connectivity issues, and hardware events.

Firewall Logs: Capture information about firewall rules, blocked traffic, and potential security threats.

DNS Logs: Record DNS queries and responses, helping to diagnose DNS-related issues and resolve domain name lookup problems.

Operating System Logs: Logs generated by the underlying operating system to report system events, errors, and resource utilisation.

System Logs: Include information about system startup, shutdown, hardware errors, and kernel-level events.

Cloud Service Logs: Logs generated by cloud providers (e.g., AWS CloudWatch, Azure Monitor) to monitor and manage cloud resources and services.

Resource Activity Logs: Track resource provisioning, scaling, and configuration changes in cloud environments.

Application Performance Logs: Capture metrics related to cloud-based applications, serverless functions, and containerised services.

Debug Logs: Provide granular information about application processes, variables, and control flow to assist developers in debugging code.

Trace Logs: Capture step-by-step execution of specific functions or methods, helping developers trace issues in complex applications.

These are some common categories of logs, but the types and granularity of logs can vary widely depending on the application, system, and operational requirements. Effective log management, analysis, and retention are critical for troubleshooting, security, compliance, and operational intelligence in software and system administration.

Collecting Logs

Instrument your code to generate logs for significant events, errors, and informational messages. Log data should include context-relevant details, timestamps, and severity levels.

For example, when an error occurs during a payment transaction, a log entry can capture the error message, stack trace, and user information for later analysis.

Leveraging Logs

Logs are a goldmine of information when it comes to investigating incidents or tracing the history of specific events. They enable you to reconstruct the sequence of activities leading up to an issue, aiding in root cause analysis and incident response.

Logs can also be used for compliance and security purposes, helping you track user activity and maintain an audit trail.

In summary, the trio of metrics, traces, and logs plays a pivotal role in achieving observability in software systems. Metrics provide real-time insights into system performance, allowing you to monitor and respond to changes swiftly. Traces offer a comprehensive view of request flow, aiding in troubleshooting and optimisation. Logs serve as a detailed record of events and errors, serving multiple purposes, from debugging to compliance.

By collecting and effectively leveraging these data types, you not only gain visibility into the inner workings of your systems but also empower your teams to proactively manage, diagnose, and enhance the reliability and performance of your software. Together, metrics, traces, and logs form a robust foundation for achieving observability excellence in the dynamic landscape of modern software development.

3.4 Techniques for Effective Data Collection

This section provides a toolbox of techniques for effective data collection. From sampling strategies to batching and aggregation methods, you'll discover how to strike a balance between comprehensive data collection and efficient resource utilisation. These techniques are vital for managing the volume of data generated by modern software systems.

Techniques for Effective Data Collection

The ability to collect and harness data effectively is paramount for achieving observability and maintaining the health and performance of applications. This section explores a toolbox of techniques for efficient data collection, these techniques are crucial for managing the voluminous data generated by modern software systems.

The Data Collection Challenge

As software systems have grown in complexity and scale, so has the volume of data generated by these systems. Monitoring, tracing, and logging mechanisms produce copious amounts of information, making it challenging to collect, process, and analyse data effectively. To address this challenge, organisations need well-defined strategies and techniques for data collection.

Sampling Strategies

Sampling is a foundational technique for managing data volume. Instead of collecting data exhaustively, sampling involves collecting a subset of data points or events at regular intervals. This approach allows for efficient data collection while providing representative insights into system behaviour.

Random Sampling: involves selecting data points or events

randomly from the entire dataset. This technique is useful when you want an unbiased representation of your data. For example, you might randomly sample HTTP requests to assess web server performance.

Periodic Sampling: involves collecting data points or events at fixed intervals. It simplifies data collection by ensuring regular and predictable data gathering. For instance, you might sample system resource utilisation metrics every minute to monitor resource trends.

Probabilistic sampling: selects data points based on a predefined probability distribution. It allows for flexible data collection, focusing on events of interest while reducing the volume of less critical data. Probabilistic sampling is commonly used in distributed tracing systems.

Adaptive sampling: adjusts the sampling rate dynamically based on system conditions or metrics thresholds. When system load is high, fewer data points are collected to reduce overhead, and vice versa. Adaptive sampling helps maintain observability in dynamic environments.

Batching and Aggregation Methods

Another effective approach to managing data volume is batching and aggregation. Instead of transmitting individual data points, events, or logs in real-time, batching groups multiple data points together, reducing the overhead of data transmission and storage.

Time-based batching: collects and transmits data points at fixed time intervals, such as every minute or hour. This technique reduces the frequency of data transmission, minimising network and storage resource usage.

Size-based batching: groups data points together until a specified batch size is reached. Once the batch size is met, the data is transmitted or processed as a single unit. Size-based batching helps optimise data transmission efficiency.

Event count aggregation: involves counting the occurrences of specific events over a defined time window. Instead of transmitting every instance of an event, only the aggregated count is sent periodically. This is commonly used in error tracking and log management.

Metrics aggregation: computes statistical measures (e.g., sum, average, percentiles) over a set of data points within a time interval. Aggregated metrics provide a high-level view of system performance while reducing the volume of raw metric data.

Filtering and Selective Collection

Not all data is equally valuable or relevant for observability. Filtering and selective data collection techniques allow organisations to focus on the most critical data while discarding less essential information.

Keyword filtering: involves collecting data that contains specific keywords, phrases, or patterns of interest. For example, you might filter logs for error messages or critical events.

Custom triggers: allow organisations to define specific conditions or thresholds that trigger data collection. For instance, data collection might be triggered when a system's CPU usage exceeds a certain threshold.

Anomaly detection: techniques identify unusual or unexpected patterns in data. When anomalies are detected, data collection can be intensified for deeper investigation. This approach is especially valuable for security monitoring and performance analysis.

Hierarchical Data Collection

In large-scale distributed systems, hierarchical data collection techniques are used to organise and prioritise data from various system components. These techniques help maintain observability without overwhelming monitoring and logging infrastructure.

Hierarchical sampling: involves sampling data at multiple levels of a system's hierarchy. For example, you might sample requests at the frontend, middle tier, and database layers to obtain a holistic view of request flow.

Aggregate hierarchies: combine data from multiple system components into higher-level aggregates. Instead of collecting data from every individual service or instance, you can collect aggregated metrics or traces from service clusters or regions.

Effective data collection is the cornerstone of observability in modern software systems. As data volumes continue to grow, organisations must adopt strategies and techniques that strike a balance between collecting comprehensive data and efficiently utilising resources. Sampling, batching, aggregation, filtering, and hierarchical data collection are essential tools in the observability toolbox, helping organisations gain actionable insights while managing the deluge of data generated by their software systems. By implementing these techniques thoughtfully, organisations can harness the power of data without drowning in it, enabling them to maintain the reliability, performance, and security of their applications and services in today's dynamic software landscape.

Hopefully now you have a solid understanding of the critical role data collection and instrumentation play in observability. You'll be equipped with the knowledge and strategies needed to set up robust data collection practices within your software systems, ensuring that you have the necessary observability data at your fingertips for analysis and troubleshooting. This knowledge prepares you for the subsequent chapters, where we explore how to make the most of the data you've collected to gain valuable insights into your systems.

Chapter 4

Metrics, Traces, and Logs

I n Chapter 4, we delve deeper into the three pillars of observability: metrics, traces, and logs. You will already have an understanding of each of these elements. However, in this chapter I will explore how these distinct data types work in concert to provide a holistic view of your software systems.

System Health

4.1 Metrics: Measuring System Health

The chapter begins by examining metrics, which are vital for monitoring the health and performance of your systems. You'll learn how metrics provide quantitative data about various aspects of your infrastructure, applications, and services. We delve into the different types of metrics, including counters, gauges, and histograms, and how to choose the right metrics for monitoring specific aspects of your system.

The Significance of Metrics

Metrics are the pulse of observability, enabling organisations to gauge the vitality and efficiency of their software systems. They transform the complex and often abstract state of systems into quantifiable values that can be tracked, analysed, and acted upon. Metrics play a multifaceted role, offering insights into performance bottlenecks, resource utilisation, error rates, and many other critical aspects of system behaviour.

Quantitative Insights

One of the primary advantages of metrics is their quantitative nature. Unlike logs or traces, which are often textual and qualitative in nature, metrics provide numerical data. This quantifiability allows for objective analysis and straightforward comparison over time, across components, or between systems.

Real-time Monitoring

Metrics are well-suited for real-time monitoring. They offer a continuous stream of data that enables organisations to detect anomalies, respond to emerging issues promptly, and make informed decisions to ensure system stability.

Trend Analysis

Over time, metrics build a historical record of system behaviour. Trend analysis involves examining how metrics change and evolve under different conditions. This historical perspective is invaluable for capacity planning, forecasting, and identifying gradual performance degradation.

Actionable Alerts

Metrics serve as the foundation for setting up actionable alerts. By establishing thresholds and triggers based on metric values, organisations can automate responses to predefined conditions, such as high CPU utilisation or a surge in error rates.

Types of Metrics

Metrics come in various flavours, each suited for specific monitoring scenarios and aspects of system behaviour. Understanding the types of metrics and when to use them is crucial for effective observability.

Counters

Counters are a fundamental type of metric used to measure the occurrence of discrete events. They are always positive and monotonically increasing, making them suitable for tracking cumulative events, such as the number of requests served or errors encountered. Counters reset to zero when the monitoring system restarts or resets.

Example: A web server might use a counter to keep track of the total number of HTTP requests it has processed.

Gauges

Gauges, in contrast to counters, represent instantaneous values at a specific point in time. They are suitable for measuring quantities that can go up or down, such as CPU usage, memory consumption, or the current number of active connections. Gauges can fluctuate and provide real-time insights into system states.

Example: Monitoring the current CPU usage percentage of a server is often done using a gauge.

Histograms

Histograms capture the distribution of values within a predefined range. They are particularly useful when dealing with data that exhibits a wide range of possible values, such as response times or request latencies. Histograms divide values into buckets or bins, allowing you to visualise data distribution and calculate percentiles.

Example: Measuring the distribution of response times for an

API endpoint helps identify outliers and understand response time variability.

Timers

Timers are a specialised type of metric used to measure the duration of events or processes. They are often paired with histograms to capture and analyse timing data. Timers are valuable for assessing the performance of critical operations, such as database queries or service response times.

Example: Timing how long it takes for a user to complete an online purchase can help optimise the checkout process.

Summary Metrics

Summary metrics combine the characteristics of gauges and histograms. They provide the mean, quantiles, and other statistical properties of a set of values, making them suitable for capturing summarised information about a metric's distribution.

Example: A summary metric might provide the average, 90th percentile, and maximum response times for an HTTP API.

Choosing the Right Metrics

Selecting the right metrics is a crucial decision in building an effective observability strategy. The choice of metrics should align with the specific goals and requirements of your monitoring and troubleshooting efforts. Here are key considerations when selecting metrics:

Relevance

Metrics should directly address the questions and concerns you have about your systems. Consider what aspects of your system's behaviour are most critical for maintaining its health and performance.

Example: If you're running a web application, monitoring

request error rates and response times may be more relevant than tracking disk usage.

Granularity

Consider the level of detail required. Should you focus on high-level system-wide metrics, or do you need fine-grained insights into individual components or services? The granularity of metrics should match your monitoring objectives.

Example: In a microservices architecture, you may need detailed metrics for each service to identify performance bottlenecks.

Thresholds and Alerts

Think about the conditions that would trigger alerts or actions. Metrics used for alerting should have clear thresholds defined, indicating when a metric value is outside the acceptable range. Consider how these thresholds align with your organisation's service-level objectives (SLOs) and the impact on end-users.

Example: If you have an SLO that specifies a maximum response time of 200 milliseconds for an API, you should set an alert threshold for response times exceeding this limit.

Historical Data

Metrics provide historical data that can be analysed to identify trends, seasonal patterns, and gradual performance changes. Think about the duration for which you need to retain historical metric data to support long-term analysis and capacity planning.

Example: If you're preparing for a holiday sales event, historical metrics data from the previous year can help anticipate traffic spikes and resource requirements.

Scalability

Consider the scalability of your chosen metrics. Will your monitoring system be able to handle the volume of data generated by the selected metrics without degrading performance or incurring excessive costs?

Example: Metrics related to user activity in a popular mobile app may generate a high volume of data points, requiring a scalable monitoring solution.

Metrics are the quantifiable essence of observability, providing real-time insights into system health and performance. They offer a structured and numerical view of complex systems, allowing organisations to monitor, analyse, and react to various aspects of their software behaviour. By understanding the significance of metrics, the different types available, and the considerations when selecting them, organisations can build a robust observability strategy that aligns with their specific goals and empowers them to maintain the reliability, efficiency, and resilience of their software systems.

4.2 Traces: Understanding Request Flow

Next, we turn our attention to traces, which offer a detailed view of request flow through your applications. Traces help you understand how requests move through microservices and dependencies, making it easier to pinpoint bottlenecks, latency issues, and errors. We explore the anatomy of trace data, the role of trace spans and traces, and how to interpret trace visualisations.

Traces: Understanding Request Flow

In the pursuit of observability within complex software systems, this section on traces takes centre stage. Traces offer a granular and comprehensive view of request flow through your applications, enabling you to navigate the intricate web of microservices, dependencies, and interactions. This section unearths the essence of trace data, the significance of trace spans and traces, and the art of deciphering trace visualisations.

The Role of Traces

Traces serve as the investigative lens into the dynamic world of request flow within your applications. They are invaluable for unravelling the intricate journey of requests as they traverse through various microservices, external dependencies, and internal components. By capturing the intricate choreography of request execution, traces empower organisations to identify bottlenecks, diagnose latency issues, and rectify errors efficiently.

Request Lifecycle Mapping

Traces are akin to breadcrumbs in the forest of request execution. They map the lifecycle of a request, providing a step-by-step account of its path from initiation to completion. This meticulous mapping enables you to comprehend the flow of requests, understand dependencies, and scrutinise each leg of the journey.

Latency Detection

Latency, the silent adversary of system performance, often lurks within the intricate layers of request execution. Traces are equipped to reveal the latency culprits by attributing time stamps to each span, allowing you to measure the time taken at each step of request processing. Armed with this data, you can diagnose delays, bottlenecks, and resource-intensive operations.

Error Diagnosis

When errors and anomalies disrupt the tranquillity of your applications, traces step in as the detective's magnifying glass. By capturing the execution context around errors, you can pinpoint the exact location of issues, trace their origins, and construct a precise diagnosis. This forensic approach streamlines troubleshooting and minimises downtime.

Anatomy of Trace Data

To fully appreciate the power of traces, it's essential to understand their anatomy—the building blocks that make up trace data.

Trace Spans

A trace is composed of individual units of work, known as spans. Each span encapsulates a specific operation or segment of a request's journey. Spans are linked together to form a trace, akin to assembling a jigsaw puzzle where each piece contributes to the complete picture.

Example: Consider a typical e-commerce application. A trace may consist of spans representing the user authentication process, product catalogue retrieval, payment processing, and response rendering.

Span Attributes

Spans are not mere placeholders; they come with a treasure trove of attributes. These attributes provide context and metadata about the span, making it easier to understand the operation it represents. Attributes can include timestamps, resource information, error codes, and more.

Example: For a span representing a database query, attributes may include the SQL statement, the database server's address, and the query execution time.

Trace Context

Trace spans are not isolated entities; they are part of a broader narrative—the trace itself. Trace context carries essential information across spans, including trace and span identifiers. This contextual thread binds spans together, ensuring they collectively narrate the story of a request's journey.

Example: Imagine a user's journey through a mobile application: authenticating, browsing products, and placing an order. Trace context ensures that spans across different services and components are linked, providing a holistic view of the user's interactions.

The Role of Visualisation

Traces generate vast volumes of data, and making sense of this data requires effective visualisation techniques. Trace visualisations provide a graphical representation of the request flow, making it easier to comprehend and analyse complex interactions.

Trace Tree View

The trace tree view is a common visualisation technique that arranges spans in a hierarchical tree structure. It offers a chronological representation of spans, illustrating the order of execution and the relationships between them.

Example: In a trace tree view, you can see that the authentication span precedes the product catalogue retrieval span, and both are part of the larger order placement span.

Gantt Chart

The Gantt chart visualisation resembles a timeline, displaying spans as horizontal bars with timestamps. This view provides a clear depiction of the time taken by each span and allows for easy identification of latency issues.

Example: A Gantt chart visualisation reveals that the database query span took significantly longer to execute compared to other spans in the trace.

Waterfall Chart

The waterfall chart is a variation of the Gantt chart, providing a visual representation of the sequential execution of spans. It helps identify dependencies and visualise the flow of requests through various services and components.

Example: A waterfall chart can show that the user authentication span must complete before the product catalogue retrieval span can start.

Interpreting Trace Visualisations

While trace visualisations are powerful tools, interpreting them effectively requires a keen eye and an understanding of the underlying principles.

Latency Identification

Visualisations highlight spans with extended durations, allowing you to spot latency hotspots. A prolonged span in the trace tree or Gantt chart may indicate a bottleneck or resource-intensive operation.

Example: An extended span in the trace visualisation may indicate that a database query is taking longer to execute than expected.

Error Tracking

Trace visualisations often incorporate colour-coding to signify

4.3 Logs: Capturing Detailed Events

Logs, as the third pillar of observability, provide a rich source of detailed event and error data. This section explains the significance of structured logging and how to make the most of log data. We discuss log aggregation, search, and analysis techniques to turn raw log entries into actionable insights.

The Essence of Logs

Logs are the textual narrators of your software's journey, capturing every event, error, and action as it unfolds. They serve as the documentary evidence of your application's life, making them indispensable for understanding what happened, when it happened, and why it happened.

Event Documentation

At their core, logs are the story keepers of your software. They document each event, whether it's a user login, a database query, or an application error. By meticulously recording these events, logs enable you to reconstruct the past and gain insights into system behaviour.

Error Identification

Logs are the detectives in the realm of observability, specialising in error identification. When issues arise, logs are your trusty allies, providing the clues needed to track down errors, pinpoint their origins, and devise strategies for resolution.

Troubleshooting Toolkit

Logs are the toolkit for troubleshooting. When things go awry, logs are your Swiss Army knife, armed with data to analyse, patterns to discover, and anomalies to uncover. They are the foundation of effective debugging and issue resolution.

Structured Logging

While logs can be a goldmine of information, their true value is unlocked when structured properly. Structured logging involves formatting log entries in a consistent, machine-readable manner. This structured approach enhances searchability, analysis, and automation of log data.

Key-Value Pairs

One of the fundamental techniques in structured logging is the use of key-value pairs within log entries. Instead of unstructured text, log messages are composed of fields with clear keys and corresponding values.

Example: A traditional log entry might be: `Error: User login failed for user_id=12345`. In structured logging, it becomes: `{"level": "error", "message": "User login failed", "user_id": 12345}

Log Schemas

Log schemas define the structure and format of log entries, establishing a common language for log data. Schema validation ensures that logs adhere to predefined formats, making them predictable and easier to analyse.

Example: A log schema might specify that every log entry must include fields like `timestamp`, `severity`, and `message`.

Benefits of Structured Logging

Structured logging brings several benefits to the table:

Searchability: Key-value pairs enable efficient searching and filtering of log data. You can quickly find specific events or errors by querying fields like `user_id` or `error_code`.

Consistency: Structured logs follow a standardised format, ensuring consistency across log entries. This consistency simplifies log processing and analysis.

Automation: Machine-readable logs facilitate automation. Log entries with clear structures can be parsed and processed by automated tools, enabling actions like alerting and reporting.

Log Aggregation

As your applications generate a deluge of log entries, managing them becomes a daunting task. Log aggregation steps in as the solution, consolidating log data from multiple sources into a central repository.

Centralised Log Storage

Log aggregation platforms, such as Elasticsearch, Logstash, and Kibana (ELK Stack), or cloud-based services like AWS CloudWatch Logs, provide centralised storage for log entries. They act as a hub where logs from various components and services converge.

Example: In a microservices architecture, logs from different services are aggregated into a centralised system for unified monitoring.

Benefits of Log Aggregation

Log aggregation offers several advantages:
Single View: Aggregated logs provide a single view of application events, making it easier to track issues across the entire system.

Scalability: Log aggregation platforms can scale to handle vast amounts of log data, ensuring they can keep up with your application's growth.

Retrieval: Aggregated logs are readily accessible, simplifying the process of retrieving log entries for analysis and investigation.

Log Search and Analysis

Centralised log storage is just the beginning. To derive actionable insights from log data, you need effective search and analysis capabilities.

Query Language

Log aggregation platforms typically provide a query language that allows you to search log entries based on specific criteria, such as keywords, time ranges, or field values. These queries help you find relevant log entries efficiently.

Example: You can use a query to search for all log entries with a severity level of "error" within the last 24 hours.

Alerting

Alerting mechanisms in log aggregation platforms enable proactive monitoring. You can define alert rules based on specific log patterns or conditions. When a matching log entry is detected, the system triggers an alert, allowing you to respond promptly.

Example: An alert rule can be set to notify administrators when the error rate exceeds a certain threshold.

Log Analysis Tools

Beyond basic searching, log aggregation platforms often provide log analysis tools and dashboards. These tools offer visualisations, trend analysis, and anomaly detection, helping you derive meaningful insights from log data.

Example: A log analysis dashboard might display error trends over time or highlight unusual patterns in log data.

Log Retention and Archiving

While logs are essential for real-time monitoring and troubleshooting, they can also consume significant storage resources over time. Log retention and archiving strategies help you strike a balance between historical data preservation and resource optimisation.

Log Retention Policies

Log retention policies define how long log data should be retained in the central storage. These policies are based on regulatory requirements, operational needs, and storage capacity constraints.

Example: A retention policy might specify that logs should be kept for 30 days for operational purposes and archived for seven years for compliance reasons.

Log Archiving

Log archiving involves moving older log data to long-term storage, such as archival storage or cold storage. Archiving helps free up resources in the central log storage while preserving historical data for compliance or historical analysis.

Example: Log entries older than 90 days might be automatically archived to a less expensive, long-term storage solution.

Logs are the unsung heroes of observability, providing a detailed account of every event and error in your software systems. By embracing structured logging, log aggregation, and robust search and analysis techniques, organisations can transform logs from raw textual records into actionable insights. These insights empower you to monitor system behaviour, diagnose issues, and troubleshoot with precision, ensuring the reliability, performance, and security of your applications in today's complex software landscape.

4.4 Synergy of Metrics, Traces, and Logs

One of the key takeaways from this section is how metrics, traces, and logs complement each other. We demonstrate how combining these data types can provide a 360-degree view of your system's behaviour, making it easier to troubleshoot complex issues, identify performance bottlenecks, and detect anomalies effectively.

Unified Insights

Metrics, traces, and logs each bring their unique strengths to the observability table. While metrics offer quantitative insights into system health, traces delve deep into request flow, and logs capture detailed events and errors. By combining these data types, organisations can achieve a 360-degree perspective on their software systems.

Performance Bottleneck Detection

Consider a scenario where you notice a spike in response time for a critical service in your application. Metrics can highlight the overall performance degradation, indicating that something is amiss. However, to identify the root cause, traces come into play. Traces allow you to follow the journey of individual requests through various microservices and dependencies, revealing precisely where latency is introduced.

Example: Metrics indicate a 30% increase in response time for an e-commerce application. Traces reveal that the bottleneck occurs in the payment processing service, not in the frontend or database.

Anomaly Detection

Anomalies in system behaviour can be elusive, often manifesting as subtle deviations from the norm. Metrics are adept at flagging abnormal patterns in numerical data, such as sudden spikes in CPU utilisation. However, logs play a vital role in providing contextual information about these anomalies.

Example: Metrics detect a sharp increase in error rates. Logs associated with the same timeframe reveal that the errors are related to a specific database query, helping pinpoint the problematic code.

Troubleshooting Complex Issues

Complex issues, which involve multiple components and interactions, are challenging to diagnose with a single data type. Metrics may indicate a general system instability, but understanding the precise sequence of events and the context in which errors occurred is where traces and logs shine.

Example: An e-commerce platform experiences intermittent checkout failures. Metrics show a rise in error rates. Traces uncover that the issue arises when third-party payment gateway calls time out. Logs reveal that the timeout is caused by an intermittent network issue with the payment provider.

Correlation and Context

The synergy of metrics, traces, and logs extends beyond their individual capabilities. It's the correlation and context they provide when viewed together that truly amplify observability.

Cross-Referencing

By cross-referencing metrics, traces, and logs, organisations can validate their observations. Metrics may indicate a drop in throughput, while traces and logs help confirm whether it's due to an increase in request processing times or a decrease in incoming requests.

Example: Metrics show a drop in request throughput. Traces reveal that the slowdown is due to a bottleneck in the authentication service. Logs confirm that the authentication service is experiencing high CPU utilisation.

Incident Timeline Reconstruction

When a critical incident occurs, reconstructing the timeline of events is paramount. Metrics provide a high-level view of the incident's onset, traces outline the request flow, and logs provide the fine-grained details of what transpired.

Example: A service outage is detected through metrics. Traces show that the outage coincided with a deployment. Logs elucidate that the deployment script encountered an error, leading to the outage.

Root Cause Analysis

In the quest to identify the root cause of an issue, combining metrics, traces, and logs helps organisations navigate the layers of complexity. Metrics highlight the symptom, traces illuminate the affected components, and logs divulge the specifics of the issue.

Example: Metrics indicate an increase in response times. Traces reveal that the delay is introduced in the payment processing service. Logs uncover that the delay is due to a resource contention issue on the payment server.

The triumvirate of metrics, traces, and logs represents a formidable alliance in the realm of observability. These data types, when used in tandem, create a comprehensive and coherent narrative of your software systems. The synergy they offer not only enhances system monitoring but also streamlines issue diagnosis, performance optimisation, and anomaly detection.

By embracing this holistic observability approach, organisations equip themselves with the tools and insights needed to navigate the complexities of modern software systems. In a landscape where issues can be elusive and interactions intricate, the synergy of metrics, traces, and logs acts as a beacon, illuminating the path to better system health and resilience.

4.5 Standardisation and Compatibility

In this section I will introduce common formats and standards like OpenMetrics, OpenTracing, and structured logging, emphasising their role in ensuring interoperability and ease of integration with observability tools.

Standardisation and Compatibility: The Backbone of Observability

Standardisation and compatibility play pivotal roles in ensuring that metrics, traces, and logs can seamlessly work together. This section delves into the significance of adhering to common formats and standards, such as OpenMetrics, OpenTracing, and structured logging. It highlights how these standards foster interoperability and streamline the integration of observability tools, ultimately enhancing the effectiveness of observability practices.

The Need for Standardisation

Observability, in its essence, revolves around collecting,

analysing, and understanding vast amounts of data generated by software systems. Without standardised formats and protocols, this task becomes arduous and error-prone. Standardisation brings order to the chaos, creating a common language and structure for data exchange.

Interoperability

Interoperability is a key driver behind standardisation. In a diverse ecosystem of observability tools and components, it's essential that metrics, traces, and logs can flow seamlessly between systems. Standardised formats ensure that data generated by one tool can be ingested and understood by another.

Example: A metrics collection tool should be able to accept and process metrics data generated by various programming languages and frameworks without needing custom integrations for each.

Ease of Integration

Standardised data formats simplify the integration process. When all data adheres to a known standard, the effort required to connect different observability tools, agents, and libraries is significantly reduced. This makes it feasible to build a tailored observability stack that fits an organisation's unique needs.

Example: Implementing a new tracing library in your application becomes more straightforward when it adheres to the OpenTracing standard, as it can seamlessly integrate with other OpenTracing-compatible tools.
Vendor Neutrality

Standardisation promotes vendor neutrality, allowing organisations to choose the best tools for their specific requirements without locking them into proprietary formats. This flexibility ensures that investments in observability infrastructure are not tied to a single vendor's ecosystem.

Example: Using standardised log formats means that log data can be easily moved between different log management solutions without data loss or format conversion issues.

Common Observability Standards

Several standards and formats have emerged in the observability space, aiming to bring consistency and compatibility to metrics, traces, and logs.

OpenMetrics

OpenMetrics is an open standard for the exposition of metric data. It defines a common format for exposing metrics, making it easier for systems and applications to expose their performance data in a consistent way. OpenMetrics provides a structured and well-defined format for metrics, including labels and metadata.

Example: When using OpenMetrics, metrics like request latency, error rates, or resource utilisation can be exposed in a uniform format, allowing different monitoring tools to consume and analyse them without custom configurations.

OpenTracing

OpenTracing is a vendor-neutral standard for distributed tracing. It provides a set of APIs and libraries for instrumenting applications to collect and propagate trace data. OpenTracing allows developers to create traces that span multiple services and components, enabling end-to-end visibility into request flow.

Example: By adhering to the OpenTracing standard, a distributed system can generate trace data that can be seamlessly visualised and analysed by different tracing tools, regardless of their vendor.

Structured Logging

Structured logging is a practice that involves formatting log entries in a structured and machine-readable manner. While not a formal standard, structured logging conventions have gained popularity. They prescribe the use of key-value pairs within log entries to ensure consistency and ease of parsing.

Example: Adopting structured logging conventions means that log entries, whether generated by different parts of an application or different applications entirely, follow a unified format for log data.

Benefits of Standardisation

Standardisation and compatibility bring several benefits to observability practices:

Seamless Integration

Standardised data formats and protocols facilitate the integration of observability tools, reducing the effort required to set up and configure monitoring and tracing.

Example: When all components of a microservices architecture emit metrics, traces, and logs in standardised formats, aggregating and analysing data becomes a streamlined process.

Ecosystem Flexibility

Standardisation allows organisations to mix and match observability tools from different vendors, selecting the best-fit solutions for their needs without concerns about data compatibility.

Example: An organisation can choose a metrics collection tool from one vendor and a log management solution from another, knowing that they can work together seamlessly thanks to standardised formats.

Future-Proofing

Standardisation future-proofs observability investments. Organisations can be confident that their data will remain accessible and compatible with evolving tools and technologies.

Example: Data generated today in a standardised format can still be analysed and utilised effectively years down the line, even as new observability tools emerge.

In observability, standardisation and compatibility serve as the bedrock upon which effective monitoring, tracing, and logging are built. Common formats and standards, such as OpenMetrics, OpenTracing, and structured logging, not only enhance interoperability but also simplify integration efforts and promote vendor neutrality. By embracing these standards, organisations ensure that their observability practices remain agile, adaptable, and capable of providing valuable insights into the performance and health of their software systems, regardless of the tools and technologies in use.

Hopefully you now have a comprehensive understanding of the three pillars of observability: metrics, traces, and logs. You'll know how to harness each data type effectively and understand their symbiotic relationship, setting the stage for deeper analysis and problem-solving in subsequent chapters. Armed with this knowledge, you're ready to explore how to build observability into your systems, create effective visualisations, and set up meaningful alerts to monitor and improve system health.

Chapter 5

Building Observability into Microservices

C hapter 5, ventures into the world of microservices, exploring the unique challenges and opportunities that observability presents in this rapidly evolving architectural paradigm.

5.1 Microservices: A New Frontier

The chapter kicks off by providing a comprehensive overview of microservices architecture, highlighting its benefits, such as scalability and agility, as well as its inherent complexities. Here we will gain a solid understanding of the motivations behind adopting microservices and the reasons why observability is indispensable in this context.

Unveiling the World of Microservices

Microservices architecture represents a groundbreaking departure from conventional software design approaches.

Rather than constructing monolithic applications, microservices break down intricate systems into smaller, self-contained services. Each of these services is dedicated to a specific business function and communicates with others through clearly defined APIs.

Microservices

The Advantages of Microservices

Let's start by underlining the numerous advantages offered by microservices. Scalability is a pivotal benefit, allowing individual services to be autonomously scaled to handle varying workloads. This elasticity ensures optimal resource utilisation and cost-efficiency.

Another significant advantage is agility. Developers can focus on individual services, accelerating the development and deployment processes. Updates and modifications can be seamlessly implemented without affecting the entire application, reducing the risk of unintended consequences.

The Complexities Inherent to Microservices

Nevertheless, the adoption of microservices also introduces inherent complexities. Managing a distributed system comprised of microservices can be a formidable task. Each service operates independently and might employ diverse technologies and databases. Coordinating these services, ensuring their continuous availability, and effectively dealing with failures present non-trivial challenges.

The Imperative Role of Observability

This is precisely where observability emerges as an indispensable ally. Observability revolves around the practice of gaining comprehensive insights into the inner workings of a system, enabling us to comprehend the dynamics within microservices. The section underscores that observability plays a pivotal role in surmounting the hurdles posed by microservices architecture.

Understanding the Motivations Behind Microservices

To delve further into why observability is pivotal, let's delve into the motivations that prompt organisations to embrace microservices. In today's fiercely competitive digital landscape, businesses strive to innovate rapidly and respond promptly to evolving customer demands. Microservices are the vehicle that enables them to do precisely that.

Adapting to Change

Microservices empower organisations to respond effectively to change. When new features are required or specific components need updates, developers can concentrate their efforts on the relevant service. This decoupling grants independence in development and testing, diminishing the risk of disrupting the entire application.

Scalability

Scalability is a cornerstone of microservices adoption. In traditional monolithic systems, scaling typically involves augmenting resources for the entire application, even if only a fraction of it experiences heavy loads. Microservices offer the advantage of granular scalability, permitting organisations to allocate resources with precision.

Resilience

In a distributed microservices environment, failures are an inevitability. Yet, observability equips organisations with the means to detect, diagnose, and swiftly recover from these failures. It provides real-time insights into the health of services, enabling proactive measures to maintain system reliability.

Examples of Microservices

To offer a richer understanding, let's explore some concrete examples of microservices. Imagine an e-commerce platform: it might have distinct microservices for user authentication, product catalogue management, order processing, and payment handling. Each of these services can be developed, deployed, and scaled independently, enhancing flexibility and resilience.

In a social media application, microservices can handle user profiles, friend requests, notifications, and messaging, allowing for efficient development and scaling of these specific features.

In essence, microservices architecture allows complex systems to be broken down into manageable, autonomous parts, making it easier to develop, scale, and maintain intricate applications.

As our exploration of microservices and observability unfolds, we'll delve into practical strategies and tools to effectively implement observability. Let's move on for further insights and guidance on seamlessly integrating observability into the world of microservices.

5.2 Instrumenting Microservices

Observing and understanding the behaviour of microservices in a complex distributed system is a challenging task. To gain valuable insights into how microservices are performing, you must instrument them effectively. This section is dedicated to guiding you through the intricacies of instrumenting individual microservices. We'll explore how to implement observability hooks within microservices' codebases, enabling them to produce metrics, traces, and logs that are essential for gaining insight into their behaviour.

The Importance of Instrumentation

Before we dive into the technical details, let's establish why instrumentation is vital in the context of microservices.

Visibility

Instrumentation provides visibility into your microservices. Without it, you're effectively operating in the dark, with no way to monitor what's happening within your services. Metrics, traces, and logs generated through instrumentation act as your eyes and ears, allowing you to see and understand what's going on.

Debugging and Troubleshooting

When something goes wrong, as it inevitably does in a complex system, instrumentation becomes your debugging and troubleshooting toolkit. It helps you pinpoint the root causes of issues, whether it's a performance bottleneck, an error, or unexpected behaviour.

Performance Optimisation

Instrumentation also plays a critical role in performance optimisation. By collecting performance metrics, you can identify areas where your microservices may be underperforming, and then fine-tune them for optimal efficiency.

Now that we've emphasised the significance of instrumentation, let's delve into the practical aspects of implementing it within your microservices.

Implementing Observability Hooks

Observability hooks are code-level integrations that enable the collection of metrics, traces, and logs. To effectively instrument your microservices, you'll typically use observability frameworks and libraries. In this section, we'll explore how to instrument a hypothetical microservice written in Node.js using popular observability tools: Prometheus for metrics, OpenTelemetry for traces, and Winston for logging.

Instrumenting Metrics with Prometheus

Prometheus is a widely used open-source monitoring and alerting toolkit. To instrument your microservice with Prometheus, follow these steps:

Step 1: Install Prometheus Client Library

```javascript
npm install prom client
```

Step 2: Instrument Your Code

```javascript
const express   require('express');
const promClient   require('prom client');

const app   express();
const port   3000;
// Create a Prometheus Gauge metric
const gauge   new promClient.Gauge({
 name: 'http_requests_total',
 help: 'Total number of HTTP requests',
 labelNames: ['method', 'path'],
});
// Middleware to instrument incoming requests
app.use((req, res, next)    {
 gauge.labels(req.method, req.path).inc();
 next();
});

app.get('/', (req, res)    {
 res.send('Hello, World!');
});

app.listen(port, ()    {
 console.log(`App listening on port  {port}`);
});
```

In this example, we're using the Prometheus client library to create a gauge metric that tracks the total number of HTTP requests. Middleware is used to increment this gauge for each incoming request, providing valuable metrics.

Capturing Traces with OpenTelemetry

OpenTelemetry is an open-source observability framework that helps you capture traces and context information. To instrument your microservice with OpenTelemetry, follow these steps:

Step 1: Install OpenTelemetry Libraries

```javascript
npm install opentelemetry/api opentelemetry/node
```

Step 2: Instrument Your Code

```javascript
const { NodeTracerProvider } require(' opentelemetry/node');
const { SimpleSpanProcessor, ConsoleSpanExporter } require(' opentelemetry/tracing');
const { registerInstrumentations } require(' opentelemetry/instrumentation');

// Create a tracer provider
const tracerProvider new NodeTracerProvider();

// Configure span processor and exporter (console in this example)
tracerProvider.addSpanProcessor(new SimpleSpanProcessor(new ConsoleSpanExporter()));

// Register instrumentations (e.g., HTTP, Express)
registerInstrumentations({
  instrumentations: [
    // Add instrumentations relevant to your microservice
  ],
});

// Initialize the tracer
tracerProvider.register();
```

This code sets up OpenTelemetry for capturing traces in your Node.js microservice. You can further customise it to include instrumentations for specific components and libraries in your microservice stack.

Logging with Winston

Winston is a popular logging library for Node.js. To instrument your microservice for logging, follow these steps:

Step 1: Install Winston

```javascript
npm install winston
```

Step 2: Configure Winston

```javascript
const winston = require('winston');
// Create a Winston logger
const logger = winston.createLogger({
  level: 'info',
  format: winston.format.json(),
  transports: [
    new winston.transports.Console(),
  ],
});

// Example usage
logger.info('This is an info log message');
logger.error('This is an error log message');
```

Winston provides an easy way to set up logging for your microservice. You can customise the log levels, log formats, and transports as needed.

Viewing Metrics, Traces, and Logs

Instrumenting your microservices is only half the story; you also need a way to view the collected metrics, traces, and logs. Let's briefly explore some tools and techniques for doing just that.

Metrics Visualisation with Grafana

[Grafana](https://grafana.com/) is a popular open-source platform for monitoring and observability. You can integrate Grafana with Prometheus to create informative dashboards that display your microservices' metrics in real-time.

Traces Analysis with Jaeger

[Jaeger](https://www.jaegertracing.io/) is an open-source distributed tracing system that works seamlessly with OpenTelemetry. It allows you to visualise and analyse traces, helping you understand the flow of requests across your microservices.

Log Aggregation with ELK Stack

The [ELK stack](https://www.elastic.co/what-is/elk-stack) (Elasticsearch, Logstash, Kibana) is a powerful combination for log aggregation and analysis. You can use Logstash to collect logs from your microservices, Elasticsearch for indexing and storage, and Kibana for visualisation and querying.

Instrumenting microservices is a critical step in gaining observability into your complex, distributed systems. It provides the visibility, troubleshooting capabilities, and performance insights needed to maintain a reliable and efficient microservices architecture.

In summary, we have explored how to instrument a hypothetical Node.js microservice using Prometheus for metrics, OpenTelemetry for traces, and Winston for logging. These examples serve as a starting point for instrumenting your microservices, and you can customise them to suit the specific needs of your applications.

Remember that effective observability is not just about instrumenting your microservices but also about having the right tools and processes in place to analyse and act upon the data you collect. Tools like Grafana, Jaeger, and the ELK stack can help you make sense of the metrics, traces, and logs generated by your instrumented microservices, enabling you to maintain a high level of reliability and performance in your microservices architecture.

5.3 Managing Distributed Traces

Distributed tracing becomes a focal point in this section as it plays a pivotal role in understanding how requests traverse microservices. We delve into the principles of distributed tracing, exploring the concepts of spans, traces, and context propagation. Practical examples and best practices are provided to help you set up distributed tracing effectively.

Managing Distributed Traces: Unveiling the Path of Microservice Requests

In the world of microservices, understanding how requests traverse the labyrinthine network of services is a formidable challenge. This is where distributed tracing comes into play, serving as a crucial tool for dissecting and comprehending the intricate journey of requests as they hop from one microservice to another. In this section, we will immerse ourselves in the principles of distributed tracing, unravelling the concepts of spans, traces, and context propagation. To make these concepts tangible, we will provide practical examples and best practices, equipping you with the knowledge needed to set up distributed tracing effectively in their microservices ecosystem.

The Significance of Distributed Tracing

Before we embark on our journey into distributed tracing, let's grasp why it holds such a vital role in the realm of microservices.

Request Flow Visualisation

Microservices architectures often involve numerous services, each with its specific role. When a single user request or transaction traverses multiple microservices, it can become challenging to visualise the flow of that request. Distributed tracing provides a clear picture of how requests move across these services, making it invaluable for debugging and performance optimisation.

Latency Identification

In a distributed system, pinpointing the source of latency or performance bottlenecks is like searching for a needle in a haystack. Distributed tracing allows you to identify precisely which microservice is responsible for delays, enabling you to optimise your system effectively.

Troubleshooting and Debugging

When things go wrong, and they inevitably do, distributed tracing serves as a detective's toolkit. It helps you trace back the steps of a request and identify where errors occurred or where exceptions were thrown, significantly reducing the time required for troubleshooting.

Core Concepts of Distributed Tracing

1. Spans

Spans are the fundamental building blocks of distributed tracing. A span represents a single unit of work, typically associated with a specific operation within a microservice. For example, when a user makes an HTTP request to a microservice, that operation can be represented as a span. Spans have essential attributes such as a start time, duration, and a unique identifier.

2. Traces

A trace is a collection of spans that represent a complete journey of a request as it flows through various microservices. Traces connect spans together, forming a chronological sequence that tells the story of how a request traversed the microservices ecosystem. A trace typically starts with an incoming request and ends with a response to that request.

3. Context Propagation

Context propagation is the mechanism that allows trace information to be passed between microservices as requests flow through them. It ensures that each microservice involved in processing a request can add information to the trace and pass it along to the next microservice. Context propagation is crucial for stitching spans together to form a complete trace.

Practical Examples of Distributed Tracing

Let's bring these abstract concepts to life with practical examples using well-known distributed tracing tools, Jaeger and OpenTelemetry.

Setting Up Jaeger for Distributed Tracing

Step 1: Install and Run Jaeger

To get started with Jaeger, you need to install and run the Jaeger backend components, including the Jaeger Collector, Jaeger Query, and Jaeger Agent. You can find detailed installation instructions on the [Jaeger website](https://www.jaegertracing.io/docs/latest/getting-started/).

Step 2: Instrument Your Microservices

Instrument your microservices to send trace data to Jaeger. In this example, we'll use Node.js and the OpenTelemetry library to instrument a Node.js-based microservice.

```javascript
const { NodeTracerProvider }  require(' opentelemetry/node');
const { SimpleSpanProcessor, ConsoleSpanExporter } require(' opentelemetry/tracing');
```

```javascript
const { JaegerExporter }    require(' opentelemetry/exporter
jaeger');

const provider    new NodeTracerProvider();

// Configure Jaeger exporter
const jaegerExporter    new JaegerExporter({
  serviceName: 'my microservice',
  agentUrl:   'http://jaeger agent:6831',   //   Jaeger   Agent
endpoint
});

// Set up span processing and export
provider.addSpanProcessor(new
SimpleSpanProcessor(jaegerExporter));
provider.addSpanProcessor(new          SimpleSpanProcessor(new
ConsoleSpanExporter()));

provider.register();
```

This code configures OpenTelemetry to export traces to Jaeger for a microservice named 'my-microservice'. Make sure to adjust the `serviceName` and `agentUrl` according to your setup.

Step 3: Start Tracing Spans

Instrument your microservice code to start tracing spans for relevant operations. For example:

```javascript
const          tracer                 require(' opentelemetry/
api').trace.getTracer('my microservice');

function processRequest(req, res) {
  const span    tracer.startSpan('processRequest');
  // Your microservice logic here
  span.end();
  res.send('Request processed');
}
```

In this example, we create a span for the 'processRequest' operation and end it when the operation is complete.

Visualising Traces in Jaeger

Once you've set up Jaeger and instrumented your microservices, you can use the Jaeger UI to visualise traces. Access the Jaeger UI in your web browser (usually at http://localhost:16686) and search for traces related to your microservices. You'll see a graphical representation of how requests flow through your services, with detailed information about each span.

Best Practices for Distributed Tracing

To ensure that your distributed tracing implementation is effective, consider the following best practices:

1. Consistency in Span Names

Use consistent and meaningful span names across your microservices. Naming conventions such as "HTTP request" or "Database query" make it easier to understand traces and identify bottlenecks.

2. Add Contextual Information

Include relevant context information in your spans, such as user IDs, request IDs, and operation-specific details. This information enhances trace visibility and aids in debugging.

3. Sampling Strategies

Implement proper sampling strategies to avoid overwhelming your tracing system with too much data. Sampling allows you to collect traces for a subset of requests, which can be invaluable for performance analysis.

4. Error Handling

Include error information in spans when an operation encounters an error. This helps you quickly identify problematic areas in your microservices architecture.

Distributed tracing is an indispensable tool in the microservices world, providing the visibility and insights needed to understand how requests traverse complex, distributed systems. By grasping the core concepts of spans, traces, and context propagation, and by applying practical examples with tools like Jaeger and OpenTelemetry, you can set up effective distributed tracing for your microservices ecosystem.

Remember that distributed tracing is not just a technical implementation; it's a mindset that fosters a culture of observability and proactive monitoring in your microservices architecture. As you continue your journey in the world of microservices, embrace the power of distributed tracing to navigate the intricate paths of your requests with confidence.

5.4 Log Aggregation and Centralised Logging

In microservices, where applications are composed of numerous loosely coupled services and instances, logging plays a pivotal role in monitoring, diagnosing issues, and maintaining system health. However, managing logs in a microservices environment can be a daunting challenge. Logs are scattered across various services and instances, making it difficult to track the flow of requests and troubleshoot issues effectively. To address these challenges, this section focuses on log aggregation and centralised logging solutions, offering strategies and insights on how to consolidate log data. By the end of this section, you will have a comprehensive understanding of the importance of log aggregation and the practical steps to implement centralised logging in a microservices architecture.

The Complexities of Logging in Microservices

Before delving into log aggregation and centralised logging, it's crucial to recognise the complexities associated with logging in a microservices environment.

Distributed Nature: Microservices are distributed across multiple containers, virtual machines, or even different physical servers. Each microservice generates its own logs independently.

Scalability: Microservices can scale dynamically based on demand, resulting in log data that is both vast and constantly changing.

Variability: Microservices may be written in different programming languages and use various logging frameworks, making log formats and structures inconsistent.

Lack of Context: When an issue arises, tracing the flow of a request across multiple microservices can be challenging without a centralised view of logs.

Given these challenges, log aggregation and centralised logging become essential components of any robust microservices observability strategy.

Log Aggregation: A Necessity in Microservices

Log aggregation is the practice of collecting log data from various sources, such as different microservices, and consolidating it into a centralised repository. This aggregated log data forms the basis for centralised logging, providing a unified view of what's happening across the microservices ecosystem.

Advantages of Log Aggregation

Centralised Visibility: Log aggregation offers a centralised location where all logs are stored and can be accessed. This enables a single point of access for monitoring and troubleshooting.

Real-time Insights: Aggregating logs in real-time allows for immediate detection of issues and quick response to critical incidents.

Historical Analysis: Over time, aggregated logs become a valuable resource for historical analysis, helping in identifying patterns, trends, and anomalies.

Strategies for Log Aggregation

Container Logging: If your microservices run in containers (e.g., Docker), container logging tools like Docker's built-in logging or third-party solutions like Fluentd or Logstash can be used to collect logs from containers.

Log Shippers: Log shippers like Filebeat can be employed to forward logs from individual microservices instances to a centralised log aggregator.

Managed Logging Services: Cloud providers offer managed logging services like AWS CloudWatch Logs, Google Cloud Logging, and Azure Monitor. These services simplify log aggregation by providing built-in log collection and storage capabilities.

Centralised Logging Solutions

Once log data is aggregated, the next step is to implement a centralised logging solution. Centralised logging involves storing logs in a single location, often accompanied by search and visualisation tools for efficient log analysis. Let's explore some common centralised logging solutions and their benefits.

The ELK Stack (Elasticsearch, Logstash, Kibana)

The ELK Stack is a widely used open-source solution for centralised logging. It comprises:

Elasticsearch: A distributed search and analytics engine for storing and indexing log data.
Logstash: A log data processing pipeline that ingests, transforms, and sends log data to Elasticsearch.

Kibana: A visualisation and exploration tool that enables log data analysis and the creation of interactive dashboards.

The ELK Stack is highly customisable and can be tailored to specific logging requirements. It provides powerful search and visualisation capabilities, making it a preferred choice for many organisations.

Splunk (Cisco)

Splunk is a popular commercial solution for log management and analysis. It offers features like real-time indexing, search, and alerting. Splunk is known for its scalability and is often used in large enterprises with extensive logging needs.

Fluentd and Fluent Bit

Fluentd and Fluent Bit are lightweight, open-source log collectors that can forward logs to various destinations, including Elasticsearch, Amazon S3, or cloud-based logging services. They are known for their simplicity and efficiency, making them suitable for microservices environments.

Implementing Centralised Logging: Practical Steps

To implement centralised logging effectively in a microservices environment, follow these practical steps:

1. Choose a Centralised Logging Solution:

Select a centralised logging solution that best aligns with your organisation's needs and preferences. Consider factors such as scalability, cost, ease of use, and the availability of integrations.

2. Instrument Your Microservices:

Modify your microservices to include log statements. Ensure that log messages contain relevant information, including timestamps, service identifiers, and contextual data.

Example (Node.js with Winston):

```javascript
const winston    require('winston');

const logger    winston.createLogger({
  format: winston.format.json(),
  transports: [
   new winston.transports.Console(),
  ],
});

logger.info('Microservice started...');
```

3. Configure Log Shippers or Agents:

Set up log shippers or agents on each microservice instance to collect and forward log data to the chosen centralised logging solution. Configure these shippers to include the necessary metadata for context.

4. Centralised Log Storage:

Ensure that logs are stored securely and efficiently in the chosen centralised storage system. Configure retention policies to manage log data lifecycle.

5. Visualisation and Analysis:

Leverage the capabilities of your centralised logging solution to create dashboards, set up alerts, and perform log analysis. This step enables you to gain actionable insights from your log data.

6. Monitor and Iterate:

Continuously monitor your centralised logging solution's performance and effectiveness. Make necessary adjustments based on evolving requirements and changes in your microservices architecture.

In microservices, log aggregation and centralised logging are not just best practices; they are essential components of a robust observability strategy. By aggregating logs from various microservices and implementing centralised logging solutions such as the ELK Stack, Splunk, or Fluentd, organisations can gain valuable insights into their microservices ecosystem. This enables them to troubleshoot issues effectively, track the flow of requests, and ensure the health and reliability of their microservices architecture.

As you look further at the complexities of microservices, remember that centralised logging is not a one-time setup but an ongoing process. Regularly review and refine your logging strategy to meet the evolving needs of your microservices environment. With a well-implemented centralised logging solution in place, you'll be better equipped to handle the challenges and opportunities that come with the microservices paradigm.

5.5 Challenges and Benefits of Observing Microservices

Microservices architecture has transformed the way we design and build software systems, enabling organisations to achieve unprecedented scalability and agility. However, with these advantages come unique challenges in the realm of observability. In this section, we candidly explore the challenges that microservices present for observability, such as maintaining context across services, dealing with high cardinality metrics, and managing the sheer volume of observability data generated in a distributed environment. Despite these challenges, we'll also delve into the substantial benefits that observability brings to the table, including faster troubleshooting, improved performance optimisation, and enhanced system reliability.

The Challenges of Observing Microservices

1. Maintaining Context Across Microservices:

In a microservices architecture, a single user request can traverse multiple services, each with its own logs, metrics, and traces. Maintaining context across these services to understand the complete journey of a request is a significant challenge. Without proper context propagation and aggregation, tracing the flow of a request becomes akin to assembling a puzzle without all the pieces.

2. High Cardinality Metrics:

Microservices can generate a vast number of metrics due to their dynamic nature. Each service instance may produce unique metrics, resulting in high cardinality. High cardinality metrics can strain monitoring and storage systems, making it challenging to efficiently process and analyse the data.

3. Managing Observability Data Volume:

In a distributed microservices environment, the volume of observability data generated can be overwhelming. Logs, traces, and metrics from multiple services and instances inundate monitoring tools, potentially leading to performance bottlenecks and increased operational costs.

4. Instrumentation Complexity:

Instrumenting microservices for observability requires a level of complexity that can be daunting. Developers must embed observability hooks into each service, which can be time-consuming and error-prone. Furthermore, ensuring that these hooks provide consistent and meaningful data across services can be a challenge.

5. Dynamic Scaling:

Microservices often scale dynamically in response to varying workloads. This dynamic scaling complicates observability as the number of service instances can change rapidly. Ensuring that all instances are properly instrumented and monitored is a continual challenge.

The Benefits of Observability in Microservices

While microservices introduce these challenges, they also bring forth a host of benefits when it comes to observability. Let's explore the substantial advantages that observability provides in the context of microservices.

1. Faster Troubleshooting:

Observability enables rapid issue detection and troubleshooting. With centralised logs, traces, and metrics, pinpointing the root cause of problems becomes more efficient. Developers can quickly identify which service or component is responsible for issues and take immediate corrective action.

2. Improved Performance Optimisation:

Microservices observability empowers organisations to optimise performance proactively. By analysing performance metrics and traces, you can identify bottlenecks, latency issues, and resource constraints. This information allows for targeted optimisations, resulting in a more responsive and efficient system.

3. Enhanced System Reliability:

Reliability is a cornerstone of microservices. Observability plays a vital role in maintaining system reliability by providing real-time insights into service health and uptime. It allows for proactive monitoring and alerting, enabling organisations to address issues before they impact users.

4. Scalability with Confidence:

Microservices can scale effortlessly, and observability ensures that you can scale with confidence. By monitoring key performance indicators (KPIs) and resource utilisation, you can make informed decisions about when and how to scale your services to meet user demand efficiently.

5. Data-Driven Decision-Making:

Observability data provides a wealth of information that can inform decision-making processes. It allows organisations to make data-driven choices about infrastructure optimisation, feature prioritisation, and resource allocation, ultimately leading to more strategic and efficient operations.

Overcoming Challenges: Best Practices

To harness the benefits of observability in microservices while addressing the challenges, consider the following best practices:

1. Standardise Observability Tools:

Standardise the use of observability tools and frameworks across your microservices ecosystem. Consistency in tools simplifies the monitoring and analysis process, making it easier to manage and troubleshoot.

2. Implement Context Propagation:

Use context propagation techniques to maintain context across microservices. Implement distributed tracing solutions like OpenTelemetry to trace the flow of requests seamlessly across services, enabling end-to-end visibility.

3. Sampling Strategies:

Implement sampling strategies to manage high cardinality metrics. Sampling allows you to collect observability data for a subset of requests, reducing the volume of data while still capturing essential insights.

4. Data Retention Policies:

Establish data retention policies for observability data. Define how long you need to retain logs, traces, and metrics and configure your monitoring tools accordingly to manage data storage and costs effectively.

5. Automated Instrumentation:

Explore automated instrumentation solutions that can simplify the process of embedding observability hooks into your microservices. Tools like auto-instrumentation libraries can reduce the burden on developers.

6. Dynamic Scaling Considerations:

When dealing with dynamic scaling, ensure that observability tools and configurations can adapt to changes in the number of service instances. Auto-discovery mechanisms and dynamic configuration updates can help maintain observability during scaling events.

Observing microservices presents both challenges and substantial benefits. The distributed nature of microservices can complicate observability, leading to issues with context maintenance, high cardinality metrics, and data volume management. However, with the right strategies and tools, these challenges can be addressed effectively.

The benefits of observability in a microservices architecture cannot be understated. Faster troubleshooting, improved performance optimisation, enhanced system reliability, and data-driven decision-making all contribute to the success of microservices-based applications.

As organisations continue to embrace microservices, they must invest in robust observability practices to navigate the complexities of this architectural paradigm successfully. By doing so, they can unlock the full potential of microservices while ensuring the reliability and performance of their systems. In the ever-evolving world of microservices, observability remains an essential compass for organisations on their journey toward agility and innovation.

You should now have a deeper understanding of how observability applies specifically to microservices architectures. They'll be equipped with the knowledge and practical insights needed to effectively instrument and observe microservices, making it possible to gain valuable insights into the behaviour and performance of individual services and the entire microservices ecosystem. This knowledge is a crucial stepping stone as we continue our journey through the world of observability.

Chapter 6

Visualisation and Dashboards

T his chapter opens by highlighting the power of data visualisation in the observability landscape. It emphasises how well-designed visualisations can distil complex data into easily digestible forms, enabling teams to quickly identify trends, anomalies, and performance issues.

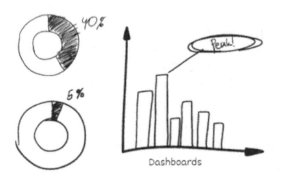

Dashboards

6.1 The Power of Data Visualisation

Data Visualisation

Organisations collect vast amounts of data, but this wealth of information is only as valuable as our ability to understand and interpret it. This is where data visualisation steps into the spotlight, playing a pivotal role in transforming raw data into actionable insights. The opening chapter of our exploration into data visualisation begins by highlighting its profound impact in the observability landscape, shedding light on how this transformative tool can distil complex data into easily digestible forms. It is a force that enables teams to swiftly identify trends, anomalies, and performance issues, ultimately revolutionising decision-making processes.

Data visualisation is the art of presenting data in a graphical or visual format, making it more accessible and comprehensible to a wide range of audiences. At its core, it transforms rows and columns of numbers and statistics into charts, graphs, and diagrams that tell a compelling story. The power of data visualisation lies in its ability to simplify complexity, turning data into a language that humans can easily understand and act upon.

In the observability landscape, which encompasses fields as diverse as business analytics, healthcare, finance, and technology, data visualisation serves as a critical tool for gaining insights into intricate systems and processes. This section underscores the importance of well-designed visualisations, which serve as windows into the inner workings of these complex systems. These visualisations act as a bridge between the data and the decision-makers, enabling them to navigate through the information maze with ease.

One of the most significant advantages of data visualisation is its capacity to reveal trends. Patterns that might remain hidden in tables of numbers become glaringly obvious when presented graphically. For instance, a line chart tracking monthly sales figures can quickly reveal seasonal fluctuations or long-term growth trends. This newfound understanding allows organisations to make data-driven decisions, optimising their strategies for maximum impact.

Furthermore, data visualisation excels at highlighting anomalies. Anomalies can be subtle deviations from the norm or glaring outliers, and they often carry valuable insights or point to potential issues. Heatmaps, scatter plots, and histograms can pinpoint these anomalies, prompting further investigation. In a medical context, for example, a scatter plot of patient vital signs may identify an unusual cluster of data points, signalling the need for further examination of those cases.

Performance issues are another area where data visualisation shines. Whether it's monitoring the efficiency of a manufacturing process or the response time of a website, visualisations can provide real-time feedback on performance metrics. Dashboards filled with graphs and charts enable teams to quickly identify bottlenecks or areas that require optimisation. This proactive approach can save both time and resources by addressing issues as they arise.

In addition to its analytical prowess, data visualisation has a unique ability to engage and communicate with diverse audiences. Not everyone is fluent in the language of data, but visualisations transcend linguistic and educational barriers. They provide a common ground for discussions, allowing stakeholders from different backgrounds to share insights and make informed decisions collaboratively.

Data visualisation can be a powerful storytelling tool. By presenting data in a compelling narrative, it captivates audiences and conveys complex messages effectively. This can be particularly valuable when presenting findings to executives, investors, or the general public, as it makes data relatable and persuasive.

In summary, our exploration into the power of data visualisation sets the stage for a deeper dive into this transformative tool. It underscores the significance of well-designed visualisations in the observability landscape, highlighting their ability to distil complex data into easily digestible forms. Whether uncovering trends, identifying anomalies, or addressing performance issues, data visualisation is a cornerstone of data-driven decision-making. Its universal language bridges gaps, engages audiences, and empowers organisations to harness the true potential of their data.

6.2 Creating Effective Dashboards

Effective dashboards are central to observability. This section provides a step-by-step guide on how to design and build dashboards that serve as the command centre for monitoring your systems. You'll learn best practices for layout, widget selection, and data representation to ensure that your dashboards provide real-time visibility into the health and performance of your applications and infrastructure.

Creating Effective Dashboards: Your Command Center for Observability

One crucial component stands out as the command centre for monitoring and decision-making - effective dashboards. These digital canvases serve as the visual representation of your systems' health and performance. This section offers a comprehensive step-by-step guide on how to design and construct dashboards that not only meet but exceed your observability needs. Through best practices in layout, widget selection, and data representation, you'll embark on a journey to ensure that your dashboards deliver real-time insights into the vitality of your applications and infrastructure.

Dashboards, in the context of observability, are like the cockpit of a modern jetliner. They provide the critical information and controls needed to navigate complex systems. Much like a pilot relies on their instruments, operators and decision-makers rely on dashboards to steer their organisations effectively. Hence, it is vital that these dashboards are thoughtfully designed to present information clearly and facilitate rapid decision-making.

The first cornerstone of dashboard design is layout. A well-structured layout should be intuitive, guiding the viewer's eye to the most critical information effortlessly. Key metrics and visuals should be prominently placed, with a logical flow that mirrors the workflow of the operators. Grid-based layouts are a popular choice, allowing for neat alignment of widgets, which are the individual components displaying data.

Widget selection is the next crucial step. Widgets come in various forms - from simple text displays and line charts to heatmaps and gauges. The key to success is selecting widgets that convey the right information efficiently. For instance, if you're monitoring the response times of your website, a line chart can vividly display fluctuations over time, while a gauge can instantly communicate whether performance falls within acceptable ranges.

However, widget selection isn't just about visual appeal; it's also about context. Different roles within your organisation may require different dashboards. Engineers may need technical insights into server health, while executives may prefer high-level dashboards showcasing business metrics. It's essential to tailor your widget selection to the specific needs of each user group.

Data representation is the final piece of the puzzle. How you visualise your data can significantly impact its interpretability. Data can be presented in myriad ways - bar charts, pie charts, scatter plots, and more. The choice depends on the type of data and the story you want to tell. For instance, a pie chart may be ideal for showing the composition of website traffic sources, while a bar chart could be better for comparing sales figures across different regions.

Real-time visibility is a hallmark of effective dashboards. Integrating data streams that update in real-time ensures that your dashboards provide up-to-the-minute information. This can be particularly crucial in environments where immediate action is required to address issues or capitalise on opportunities.

Dashboards should be adaptable and customisable. Users should have the flexibility to arrange widgets to suit their preferences, select the specific data they want to monitor, and set up alerts for critical events. Customisability empowers users to tailor their dashboards to their unique needs, making them more efficient in their roles.

In summary, creating effective dashboards is an art and science that plays a central role in observability. These digital command centres are instrumental in monitoring the health and performance of applications and infrastructure. Through thoughtful layout, widget selection, and data representation, you can construct dashboards that provide real-time visibility and empower decision-makers with the insights they need. Dashboards aren't just tools; they're the bridge between data and action, ensuring that your organisation sails smoothly through the seas of complexity in today's technology landscape.

6.3 Customisation and Interactivity

Modern observability tools offer a wealth of customisation options and interactivity features. Here we will discover how to tailor their dashboards to specific use cases and user roles, allowing different team members to access the data most relevant to their responsibilities. Interactivity, such as drill-down capabilities and real-time updates, further enhances the utility of dashboards.

Customisation and interactivity are essential aspects of modern observability tools, and they empower organisations to create dashboards that are not just informative but also finely tuned to meet their unique needs. Here are some examples of customisation and interactivity features that can significantly enhance the utility of dashboards:

1. User-Specific Dashboards: Modern observability tools often allow users to create their own personalised dashboards. For instance, an IT operations manager might create a dashboard focused on server health and response times, while a marketing analyst could build a separate dashboard emphasising website traffic and conversion metrics. This customisation ensures that each team member accesses the data most relevant to their role.

2. Widget Configuration: Users can typically customise individual widgets within a dashboard. They can choose which data source a widget should pull from, select the visualisation type (e.g., line chart, bar chart, heatmap), and set specific parameters, such as time ranges or filters. For example, a network engineer might configure a widget to display real-time bandwidth usage for a specific network segment.

3. Alert Thresholds: Dashboards often allow users to set up alert thresholds based on key performance indicators (KPIs). If a metric crosses a predefined threshold, the system can trigger notifications or even automate actions. For instance, an e-commerce manager can set an alert for a sudden drop in website conversion rates, enabling them to react swiftly to potential issues.

4. Drill-Down Capabilities: Interactivity features like drill-downs are immensely valuable. They enable users to explore data in more detail by clicking on specific elements within a widget. For instance, a sales manager viewing a regional sales chart can drill down to see sales data for individual stores or

even specific products within those stores.

5. Real-Time Updates: Many observability tools offer real-time data streaming, ensuring that dashboards are continuously updated with the latest information. This feature is particularly critical in scenarios where immediate action is required. For example, a network administrator monitoring network latency can see real-time updates and respond promptly to performance issues.

6. Collaborative Annotations: Collaborative features enable team members to add comments or annotations directly to the dashboard. This can serve as a valuable communication tool. For example, an incident response team can leave notes on a dashboard indicating the progress of resolving an ongoing issue, ensuring everyone is on the same page.

7. Role-Based Access Control: Customisation extends to access control. Dashboards can be configured to grant different levels of access to different user roles within an organisation. For instance, while executives may have read-only access to high-level business performance dashboards, system administrators may have full control over technical monitoring dashboards.

8. Widget Linking: Widgets can be linked to other dashboards or external resources. For example, clicking on a widget displaying server CPU utilisation could open a separate dashboard with more detailed server performance metrics or link to a knowledge base article on optimising server performance.

9. Time Series Comparisons: Users can customise dashboards to compare data over different time periods. For instance, an e-commerce website manager may want to compare website traffic and sales figures between the current month and the same month in the previous year to identify trends.

10. Geospatial Visualisation: For organisations with geographically dispersed assets or customers, interactivity can

include geospatial visualisations. Users can zoom in on maps, click on locations, and access detailed information about specific geographical areas.

Customisation and interactivity are not just features; they are the keys to unlocking the full potential of observability dashboards. These capabilities allow organisations to adapt their monitoring tools to their specific needs, empowering teams to make data-driven decisions efficiently and respond swiftly to emerging trends or issues. By tailoring dashboards and making them interactive, organisations can harness the true power of their observability tools.

Here's some examples of requirements in different IT roles. You will see the needs require specific information and insights from observability dashboards. Here are examples of what should be displayed for various IT roles:

1. Network Administrator:
   - Real-time network bandwidth utilisation.
   - Latency and packet loss metrics for critical network segments.
   - Status and performance of network devices (routers, switches, firewalls).
   - Alerts for network outages or unusual traffic patterns.

2. System Administrator:
   - Server resource utilisation (CPU, memory, disk, network) for all servers.
   - Server uptime and availability.
   - Active alerts and system health status.
   - Disk space usage and trending data.

3. Database Administrator:
   - Database query performance and response times.
   - SQL query error rates and query execution times.
   - Database server resource utilisation.

- Database connection and transaction statistics.

4. DevOps Engineer:
   - Deployment pipeline status and success/failure rates.
   - Application logs and error counts.
   - Container orchestration metrics (if using containers).
   - Infrastructure as code deployment progress.

5. Security Analyst:
   - Real-time security event alerts.
   - Anomalous user login activities.
   - Firewall and intrusion detection system (IDS) logs.
   - Vulnerability scan results and remediation progress.

6. Application Developer:
   - Application response times and error rates.
   - API usage and performance.
   - Server resource consumption by specific applications.
   - Code deployment status and version tracking.

7. IT Operations Manager:
   - High-level IT service health status.
   - Incident and outage reports.
   - Service-level agreement (SLA) compliance metrics.
   - Historical trend analysis for capacity planning.

8. Cloud Infrastructure Specialist:
   - Cloud service usage and cost monitoring.
   - Cloud resource scaling and optimisation recommendations.
   - Cloud security and compliance status.
   - Performance metrics for cloud-hosted applications.

9. Help Desk/Support Team:
   - User-reported issues and ticket status.
   - End-user device health and performance data.
   - Commonly reported error messages or issues.
   - Service desk workload and response times.

10. CIO/CTO/Executive Team:
    - High-level business KPIs (revenue, customer satisfaction).
    - IT infrastructure cost and efficiency metrics.
    - Critical incident reports and their impact on business operations.
    - Strategic technology roadmap progress and goals.

It's essential to tailor dashboards to the specific needs and responsibilities of each IT role. Customisation allows each team to focus on the data that directly affects their tasks and responsibilities, enabling them to work more efficiently and make informed decisions. Moreover, interactivity features, such as drill-down capabilities and real-time updates, provide further flexibility for users to delve deeper into the data as needed.

6.4 Alerting from Dashboards

Alerting is closely tied to dashboards in the observability ecosystem. This section explains how to set up meaningful alerts based on the data displayed on your dashboards. You'll learn about alert thresholds, notification channels, and escalation policies, ensuring that you're promptly informed when critical issues arise.

Alerting from Dashboards: Swift Responses to Critical Issues

In observability, dashboards are the visual pulse of your systems, offering real-time insights into their health and performance. However, the power of observability doesn't end with just visualising data; it extends to swift, automated responses to critical issues. This section explores the symbiotic relationship between dashboards and alerting, guiding you through the process of setting up meaningful alerts that ensure you're promptly informed when it matters most.

Alert Thresholds: Defining the Red Flags

At the core of effective alerting lies the establishment of meaningful alert thresholds. These thresholds are the red flags that signal when a particular metric or condition crosses into the danger zone. For example, if you're monitoring server CPU utilisation, you might set a threshold at 90%, indicating that anything beyond this point is cause for concern. Setting these thresholds requires a deep understanding of your systems and their acceptable operational ranges.

However, setting alert thresholds is not a one-size-fits-all endeavour. It's essential to strike a balance between sensitivity and alert fatigue. Too many alerts for minor fluctuations can lead to information overload and desensitise your team. On the other hand, setting thresholds too high might result in critical issues going unnoticed. Therefore, thoughtful consideration and periodic adjustment of alert thresholds are crucial for effective alerting.

Notification Channels: Getting the Right Message to the Right People

Once you've defined your alert thresholds, the next step is to determine how you'll receive these alerts. Notification channels play a pivotal role in this process. Common notification channels include email, SMS, mobile app push notifications, and integration with collaboration tools like Slack or Microsoft Teams.

The choice of notification channel depends on the urgency and importance of the alert and the preferences of the recipients. For instance, critical system failures might trigger SMS alerts to ensure immediate attention, while less urgent events could be sent as email notifications for later review.

Escalation Policies: Ensuring No Alert Goes Unnoticed

Escalation policies are the safety nets that ensure alerts are not missed, especially during off-hours or when the primary recipient is unavailable. These policies define a sequence of actions to be taken if an alert remains unacknowledged or unresolved for a specified period.

Typically, escalation policies start with the primary recipient, such as the on-call engineer. If they don't acknowledge the alert within a certain timeframe, the policy can escalate the alert to a secondary recipient, often a senior engineer or team lead. This escalation can continue to involve higher-level personnel until someone acknowledges and takes action on the alert.

Escalation policies are critical for maintaining the reliability and responsiveness of alerting systems, particularly in scenarios where immediate attention is needed to prevent or mitigate system downtime or data loss.

Continuous Refinement: The Key to Effective Alerting

Effective alerting is not a "set it and forget it" process. It requires ongoing monitoring, analysis, and adjustment. As your systems evolve and usage patterns change, alert thresholds may need to be fine-tuned. Reviewing the effectiveness of your alerts and escalation policies is essential to reducing false alarms and ensuring that critical issues are addressed promptly.

Furthermore, alerting should be tied closely to the data displayed on your dashboards. Dashboards provide context for alerts, enabling responders to quickly understand the situation and take appropriate action. The integration of dashboards and alerting creates a seamless workflow, where you can transition from monitoring to troubleshooting and resolution seamlessly.

In conclusion, alerting from dashboards is the bridge between observation and action in the world of observability. By setting up meaningful alert thresholds, defining appropriate notification channels, and establishing escalation policies, you can ensure that your team is promptly informed when critical issues arise. Effective alerting is not a static process but a dynamic one that requires continuous refinement and alignment with the evolving needs of your systems and organisation. Ultimately, it empowers you to respond swiftly and decisively to protect the integrity and performance of your systems and services.

Real-world Dashboard Examples
To illustrate the concepts discussed, the section presents real-world dashboard examples from various industries and use cases. These examples showcase the diverse ways in which organisations leverage observability data to monitor everything from e-commerce platforms to cloud infrastructure and IoT devices.

Continuous Improvement Through Visualisation
The section concludes by emphasising how visualisation and dashboards are not static tools but instruments for continuous improvement. Observability data, when effectively visualised, can lead to insights that drive optimisations, inform architectural decisions, and contribute to a culture of proactive system management.

Hopefully you now have a comprehensive understanding of the role of visualisation and dashboards in the observability ecosystem. They'll be prepared to create, customise, and leverage dashboards to gain valuable insights into the health, performance, and security of their systems. Armed with this knowledge, you are equipped to make data-driven decisions and take swift action in response to changing conditions in their software environments.

Chapter 7

Alerting and Anomaly Detection

I n Chapter 7, we dive into the critical realm of alerting and anomaly detection, exploring how these practices enhance your observability efforts by proactively identifying and addressing issues in your software systems.

Alerts

7.1 The Vital Role of Alerting

Let's begin by highlighting the fundamental importance of alerting in observability. Effective alerting ensures that you are promptly notified when issues or deviations from expected behaviour occur in your systems. We discuss the significance of timely response and how alerting helps mitigate potential problems before they impact users.

The Vital Role of Alerting: Safeguarding Systems and Ensuring Timely Responses

Alerting serves as the cornerstone of proactive system management and swift issue resolution. Alerting, a fundamental component of any robust observability strategy, stands as the sentinel that guards against impending threats and deviations from expected system behaviour. In this chapter, we delve into the critical role that alerting plays in ensuring the uninterrupted functionality of systems, discussing its paramount importance in facilitating timely responses and averting potential issues before they impact users.

Proactive Problem Identification: The Guardian of System Health

Alerting, at its core, acts as the vigilant guardian of system health. It is the mechanism that keeps a watchful eye on various metrics, logs, and events, ready to raise the alarm when anomalies, performance bottlenecks, or potential issues surface. These alerts serve as early warning signals, allowing IT teams to take immediate action to address the root causes of problems.

Imagine an e-commerce website that experiences a sudden surge in traffic due to a successful marketing campaign. Without effective alerting in place, the website's server infrastructure may become overloaded, resulting in sluggish performance or, worse, a complete outage. With well-defined alerts, the operations team can be instantly notified when server resources reach critical levels, enabling them to scale up the infrastructure proactively to accommodate the increased load. This proactive approach ensures that potential issues are nipped in the bud, preserving the user experience and preventing revenue loss.

Timely Responses: The Essence of Alerting

Timely responses are the heartbeat of alerting. When an alert triggers, it initiates a sequence of actions that culminate in rapid issue resolution. This sequence includes acknowledging the alert, investigating the root cause, and implementing corrective measures. The speed at which this cycle occurs can mean the difference between a minor hiccup and a major service disruption.

Consider a scenario where an online banking application detects an unusually high number of failed login attempts within a short time frame. Without timely alerting, these suspicious activities might go unnoticed until a security breach occurs. However, with effective alerting, security personnel can be immediately notified of this suspicious behaviour, enabling them to investigate and thwart potential account breaches swiftly.

Preventive Measures: Mitigating Issues Before Impacting Users

One of the most powerful aspects of alerting is its ability to facilitate preventive measures. By detecting early warning signs and triggering alerts, observability systems empower IT teams to take pre-emptive actions to mitigate issues before they cascade into user-facing problems.

For instance, consider a cloud-based service that monitors its infrastructure for resource utilisation. If an alert threshold for CPU utilisation is set, the system can trigger an alert when usage approaches critical levels. Armed with this alert, the operations team can proactively provision additional resources or optimise workloads to ensure uninterrupted service. This preemptive approach prevents slowdowns or outages that could have a direct impact on user satisfaction and business revenue.

Continuous Improvement: Evolving Alerting Strategies

Alerting is not a one-time setup; it's a dynamic process that requires continuous improvement and fine-tuning. Systems and user behaviours change over time, and as they do, alert thresholds, notification channels, and escalation policies may need adjustment.

Regularly reviewing alerting configurations, evaluating the

effectiveness of alerts, and incorporating feedback from incident post-mortems are essential practices. This iterative process ensures that alerting remains aligned with the evolving needs of your systems and organisation, keeping it effective and responsive.

In summary, this section underscores its pivotal position in observability. Alerting is not merely a feature but a lifeline that safeguards systems, enables timely responses, and empowers proactive problem mitigation. Its early warning capabilities ensure that potential issues are addressed before they impact users, preserving the integrity of services and bolstering user satisfaction. Alerting is not static; it's an ever-evolving guardian that adapts to the changing landscape of technology, ensuring the resilience and reliability of modern systems.

7.2 Setting Up Meaningful Alerts

Creating effective alerts is both an art and a science. This section provides guidance on setting up meaningful alerts that strike a balance between being informative and avoiding alert fatigue. You'll learn how to define alert conditions, thresholds, and escalation policies to ensure that alerts are actionable and relevant.

Setting Up Meaningful Alerts: Striking the Balance Between Informative and Pragmatic

The ability to set up meaningful alerts is a skill that bridges the gap between data and decisive action. Alerts serve as the sentinels of your systems, promptly notifying you when critical issues emerge. However, creating effective alerts is both an art and a science, demanding a delicate balance between providing valuable information and avoiding the dreaded phenomenon known as "alert fatigue." In this section, we delve into the intricacies of setting up alerts that not only inform but also empower you to respond promptly and effectively.

Defining Alert Conditions: Navigating the Data Stream

Alerting begins with the clear definition of alert conditions. An alert condition is the specific event or set of circumstances that should trigger an alert. It's the moment when your observability system says, "Pay attention; something needs your immediate response."

The definition of alert conditions varies widely based on your systems, applications, and objectives. Let's explore some real-world examples:

1. Server Resource Utilisation: Imagine you're responsible for managing a fleet of web servers. An appropriate alert condition in this context might be when the CPU utilisation of a server exceeds 90% for more than five minutes. This alert condition helps you proactively address potential performance bottlenecks before they impact the user experience.

2. Website Availability: For an e-commerce website, a critical alert condition might be when the site's response time exceeds eight seconds for more than three consecutive HTTP requests. Such an alert can help you quickly identify and rectify issues that could deter potential customers from making purchases.

3. Security Anomalies: In the realm of cybersecurity, alert conditions can be more complex. Suppose you're monitoring network traffic for signs of intrusion. Your alert condition might involve the detection of a series of unusual connection attempts from a single IP address within a short time frame, indicating a potential attack.

4. Application Errors: For a software development team, alerts could be triggered by specific application errors. For example, an alert condition could be defined when the application's error rate exceeds 5% of total requests in the last 15 minutes. This helps the team address critical issues promptly and maintain a high-quality user experience.

Thresholds: The Heart of Alerting Precision

Thresholds are the beating heart of alerting precision. They determine when an alert condition is met and an alert should be generated. Setting appropriate thresholds is where the art of alerting comes into play. Thresholds must be meticulously chosen to strike a balance between sensitivity and practicality.

Setting thresholds too low can result in a barrage of alerts for minor fluctuations, leading to alert fatigue and diluting the significance of genuine issues. Conversely, thresholds set too high might allow critical problems to go unnoticed until they escalate into significant incidents.

Consider these real-world examples to understand the importance of threshold selection:

1. Server Resource Utilisation: If the alert threshold for server CPU utilisation is set too low, say at 50%, you might receive frequent alerts during temporary traffic spikes, causing alert fatigue. Conversely, if the threshold is set too high, such as 98%, you risk not being alerted when the server is severely strained.

2. Website Availability: For a website, setting the response time threshold at one second might generate numerous alerts during normal fluctuations, while setting it at 30 seconds could cause delayed response to genuine issues.

3. Security Anomalies: In cybersecurity, setting the threshold for alerting on unusual login attempts too low might result in alerts for benign behaviour, while setting it too high could miss a sophisticated attack.

4. Application Errors: A low threshold for application error rates might flood your team with alerts for minor issues, while a very high threshold might lead to overlooking significant application errors.

Finding the right balance requires continuous monitoring and fine-tuning based on historical data and operational context.

Escalation Policies: Ensuring No Alert Goes Unattended

Escalation policies are the safety nets of alerting, guaranteeing that no alert goes unattended. These policies define a hierarchy of personnel or teams to be notified when an alert is generated and what actions should be taken if the alert remains unacknowledged or unresolved.

Typically, escalation policies begin with the primary recipient, often the on-call engineer or the team responsible for the affected system. If they fail to acknowledge the alert or initiate corrective action within a predefined time frame, the policy escalates the alert to a secondary recipient, such as a senior engineer or team lead. This escalation can continue to involve higher-level personnel until someone takes action to resolve the alert.

Escalation policies ensure that alerts are not only generated but also acted upon promptly, reducing the risk of issues escalating into critical incidents.

Actionable and Relevant Alerts: The End Goal

The ultimate objective of setting up meaningful alerts is to generate actionable and relevant notifications. An actionable alert provides clear guidance on the issue at hand and the steps to address it. It should answer questions such as "What is the problem?" and "What should I do about it?"

Relevance is equally crucial. Alerts should align with your organisation's objectives and the goals of the teams responsible for responding to them. An alert should never be an abstract data point but a direct indication of a condition that requires immediate attention.

Consider these examples of actionable and relevant alerts:

1. Server Resource Utilisation: An actionable alert might not only notify you that a server's CPU utilisation has crossed a threshold but also provide guidance on scaling up the server or optimising resource-intensive processes.

2. Website Availability: A relevant alert should not only inform you of a high response time but also provide insights into which specific web pages or components are affected, helping you focus your efforts on the root cause.

3. Security Anomalies: In the case of a security alert, actionable steps could include isolating the affected system, blocking suspicious IP addresses, and conducting a thorough investigation to identify the source of the intrusion.

4. Application Errors: An actionable alert for application errors should ideally include the error message, the affected component or module, and a link to relevant documentation or knowledge base articles to assist in swift troubleshooting and resolution.

In conclusion, setting up meaningful alerts is a multifaceted endeavour that combines the science of data analysis with the art of understanding your systems and their operational context. It's about defining precise alert conditions, selecting thresholds thoughtfully, and implementing escalation policies to ensure that alerts are addressed promptly. Ultimately, the aim is to generate alerts that are not just informative but actionable and relevant, empowering your teams to respond effectively and protect the integrity and performance of your systems and services.

Effective alerting is an ongoing process, requiring continuous refinement and alignment with the evolving needs of your organisation and systems. By mastering the art and science of meaningful alerts, you fortify your observability strategy, ensuring the resilience and reliability of modern technology solutions.

7.3 Anomaly Detection: Beyond Static Thresholds

Static threshold-based alerts have limitations. In this section I will introduce you to the concept of anomaly detection, a dynamic approach that leverages machine learning and statistical analysis to identify abnormal patterns and behaviours. We explore techniques for anomaly detection in metrics, traces, and logs, highlighting their benefits in pinpointing issues that may evade traditional alerting.

Anomaly Detection: Unleashing the Power of Dynamic Alerts

Static threshold-based alerts have served as the stalwart guardians of observability for years, but they have their limitations. In this section, we journey beyond the confines of rigid thresholds and introduce you to the world of anomaly detection—a dynamic approach that harnesses machine learning and statistical analysis to identify abnormal patterns and behaviours. We'll delve into techniques for anomaly detection in metrics, traces, and logs, emphasising their transformative benefits in pinpointing elusive issues that may elude traditional alerting. Additionally, we'll explore opinions and best practices to ensure you make the most of anomaly detection.

The Limitations of Static Thresholds: A Need for Evolution

Static thresholds, while straightforward to set up and understand, have notable drawbacks. They often struggle to adapt to the dynamic nature of modern IT systems and the complexities of real-world data. Here are a few of their limitations:

1. Inflexibility: Static thresholds remain fixed, unable to

accommodate fluctuations in data that are perfectly normal but fall outside predefined limits. This can lead to a flood of false positives or, conversely, missed anomalies.

2. Manual Tuning: Continuously adjusting static thresholds to strike the right balance between sensitivity and specificity can be labour-intensive and often reactive rather than proactive.

3. Context Blindness: Static thresholds lack the ability to consider the context in which an alert condition occurs. What might be an anomaly at one time could be entirely normal during another period.

4. Data Diversity: Modern observability generates a vast array of data types, from metrics and traces to logs. Static thresholds alone struggle to handle this diversity effectively.

Enter Anomaly Detection: A Dynamic Approach

Anomaly detection introduces dynamism to the alerting process. Instead of relying on fixed thresholds, it leverages advanced techniques to model the expected behaviour of your systems over time. Deviations from this expected behaviour trigger alerts. Here's why anomaly detection is a game-changer:

1. Adaptability: Anomaly detection models adapt to changing conditions, recognising that what's normal can vary by time of day, day of the week, or seasonality. This adaptability reduces false positives and helps identify genuine anomalies.

2. Context Awareness: Machine learning-based anomaly detection incorporates context, considering historical patterns and dependencies between metrics. It can distinguish between a harmless traffic spike during a marketing campaign and a potential server overload.

3. Data Variety: Anomaly detection techniques can be applied to various data types, from numerical metrics to structured logs and even unstructured text. This flexibility allows for a more

comprehensive understanding of system behaviour.

4. Early Detection: Anomaly detection can spot emerging issues before they manifest as critical incidents. This proactive approach enables teams to address problems in their infancy, preventing widespread impact.

Best Practices for Anomaly Detection

While anomaly detection opens new horizons in observability, implementing it effectively requires careful consideration and adherence to best practices:

1. Data Preparation: Ensure your data is clean, well-structured, and free from outliers. Preprocessing steps, such as normalisation and filtering, can enhance the accuracy of anomaly detection models.

2. Feature Engineering: Select relevant features or metrics for modelling. Consider domain knowledge and historical trends when choosing input variables.

3. Training Data: Use a sufficiently large and representative dataset for model training. Incorporate historical data to capture seasonality and long-term trends.

4. Evaluation: Continuously evaluate the performance of your anomaly detection models using metrics like precision, recall, and F1-score. Adjust model parameters as needed to strike the right balance between false positives and false negatives.

5. Human-in-the-Loop: While automation is valuable, human expertise remains critical. Integrate anomaly detection alerts into your incident response workflows, where human judgement can validate and contextualise alerts.

6. Feedback Loops: Implement feedback loops to continuously improve your models. Monitor false positives and negatives, and fine-tune your algorithms accordingly.

7. Interdisciplinary Collaboration: Foster collaboration between data scientists, domain experts, and IT operations teams. Combining technical knowledge with subject matter expertise enhances the effectiveness of anomaly detection.

The Future of Observability

In observability, embracing anomaly detection represents a critical step toward proactive and efficient system management. As data complexity continues to grow, static threshold-based alerts alone become increasingly inadequate. The ability to adapt to changing conditions, consider context, and detect emerging issues early on is paramount.

Anomaly detection, powered by machine learning and statistical analysis, empowers organisations to stay ahead of the curve, swiftly addressing issues before they escalate into full-blown incidents. It's a testament to the marriage of human expertise and technological innovation, where the art of observability meets the science of data analysis.

As organisations navigate the complexities of modern IT ecosystems, anomaly detection emerges as a beacon of progress. By moving beyond static thresholds and embracing dynamic, context-aware alerting, you unlock the potential to proactively safeguard your systems, enhance user experiences, and embrace a future where observability is not just about reacting to issues but predicting and preventing them.

7.4 Notification Channels and Incident Management

In the world of alerting, how alerts are communicated and managed is as crucial as their creation. We delve into notification channels, including email, chat platforms, and incident management tools. You will gain insights into how to streamline incident response processes, ensuring that the right team members are informed, and that issues are resolved efficiently.

Notification Channels and Incident Management: Orchestrating Effective Responses

The effectiveness of alerting doesn't end with the creation of alerts. Equally vital is how these alerts are communicated and managed. This section delves into the crucial aspects of notification channels and incident management, emphasising the pivotal role they play in streamlining incident response processes, ensuring prompt and efficient issue resolution, and keeping the right team members informed.

Diverse Notification Channels: Reaching the Right Audience

Notification channels are the conduits through which alerts traverse from the monitoring system to the incident response teams. These channels serve as the arteries of observability, ensuring that alerts are disseminated to the right people at the right time. Here are some key notification channels:

1. Email: Email notifications are a ubiquitous and versatile choice for alert dissemination. They provide a record of alerts and offer the flexibility to reach team members across different time zones.

2. Chat Platforms (e.g., Slack, Microsoft Teams): Collaboration tools have become central to modern incident management. Integrating alert notifications with chat platforms fosters real-time communication and facilitates swift incident collaboration.

3. SMS/Text Messages: For critical alerts that demand immediate attention, SMS notifications ensure that team members are informed, even when they are away from their desks.

4. Mobile App Push Notifications: Mobile app notifications are indispensable for on-call personnel who need to stay connected

while on the go. They ensure alerts are never missed, regardless of location.

5. Voice Alerts: In extreme scenarios, such as system outages, automated voice calls can be used to escalate alerts, ensuring that they reach the right personnel urgently.

Incident Management Tools: Orchestrating Responses

Incident management tools serve as the command centres for incident response teams. They play a pivotal role in orchestrating responses by consolidating alerts, providing context, and facilitating collaboration among team members. Here's why they're indispensable:

1. Centralised Incident Dashboard: Incident management tools offer a centralised dashboard where all alerts and incidents are aggregated. This single pane of glass provides a holistic view of ongoing issues, allowing teams to prioritise and respond accordingly.

2. Alert Triage and Assignment: These tools automate the triage process by assigning alerts to the appropriate on-call personnel based on predefined rules and rotations. This ensures that incidents are promptly addressed by the right experts.

3. Incident Tracking: Incident management tools enable teams to track the entire incident lifecycle, from alert creation to resolution. This documentation is invaluable for post-incident analysis and continuous improvement.

4. Collaboration Features: Collaboration is at the heart of effective incident response. These tools offer chat and communication integrations, enabling team members to collaborate in real time, share insights, and work together to resolve incidents efficiently.

5. Escalation and Acknowledgment: Automated escalation policies can be configured within these tools, ensuring that

alerts are escalated to higher-level personnel if they remain unacknowledged or unresolved. This prevents alerts from slipping through the cracks.

Effective incident management is more critical than ever. Organisations that invest in robust notification channels and incident management tools are better equipped to respond swiftly and decisively to issues, minimising downtime and ensuring a seamless user experience.

In summary, observability is not solely about generating alerts; it's about orchestrating responses. Notification channels and incident management tools are the linchpins that connect data to action, ensuring that the right individuals are informed promptly and incidents are resolved efficiently. By embracing these components, organisations fortify their ability to navigate the intricate landscape of modern IT systems, ultimately delivering reliability and satisfaction to their users.

7.5 Monitoring the Monitors: SLOs and SLIs

To maintain a high level of observability, it's essential to monitor the effectiveness of your alerting and observability tools themselves. We introduce Service Level Objectives (SLOs) and Service Level Indicators (SLIs) as mechanisms for measuring the reliability of your observability stack. These concepts help ensure that your monitoring and alerting infrastructure remains robust.

"Monitoring the Monitors: SLOs and SLIs" is a crucial aspect of maintaining a robust observability ecosystem. This practice revolves around measuring the reliability and effectiveness of your alerting and observability tools to ensure that they remain dependable. Two key concepts in this realm are Service Level Objectives (SLOs) and Service Level Indicators (SLIs). Let's explore these concepts with examples and use cases.

Service Level Objectives (SLOs)

SLOs are specific, measurable goals that define the level of service quality you aim to provide. They set the standard for the reliability and performance of your observability tools. SLOs typically include:

1. Service: The system or component you are monitoring.
2. Metric: The performance metric that represents the desired service level.
3. Target: The acceptable level of performance, often expressed as a percentage.

Example SLO:
Service: Website Uptime
Metric: Availability
Target: 99.9% uptime per month

Use Case: In the context of observability, you can establish SLOs for various aspects of your monitoring stack, such as the uptime of your monitoring server, the responsiveness of your alerting system, or the accuracy of your anomaly detection models.

Service Level Indicators (SLIs)

SLIs are specific, quantifiable measurements of the service's performance. They are the real-world metrics you use to assess whether your SLOs are being met. SLIs should closely reflect the user experience.

Example SLI:
Service: Website Uptime
Metric: HTTP Response Status Code 200 (OK) rate

Use Case: In this case, the SLI measures the percentage of HTTP requests that return a 200 (OK) status code. If the SLI consistently falls below the SLO's target (e.g., 99.9% uptime), it indicates a potential issue with your monitoring stack's ability to capture and report on website uptime accurately.

Use Cases for Monitoring the Monitors with SLOs and SLIs

1. Alerting System Reliability: SLOs and SLIs can be applied to your alerting system. For instance, you can set an SLO for the responsiveness of your alerting system and use SLIs like alert delivery time or false positives rate to measure its performance. If your SLO isn't met, it's a sign that your alerting system might not be reliable.

2. Data Collection Accuracy: In observability, data accuracy is critical. You can establish SLOs around the accuracy of collected metrics or log data. SLIs here could include data completeness or data loss rates. If these SLIs deviate from the SLO, it indicates potential issues with data collection.

3. Dashboard Performance: SLOs and SLIs can also be applied to the performance of your observability dashboards. For instance, you can set an SLO for dashboard load times and use SLIs like average load time or responsiveness during traffic spikes to measure performance. This helps ensure that users can access critical data without delays.

4. Anomaly Detection Precision: If you use anomaly detection models in your observability stack, SLOs and SLIs can assess their precision. For example, an SLO could specify that 95% of alerts generated by anomaly detection should be true positives, while SLIs measure the true positive and false positive rates.

5. Incident Management Efficiency: Assess the efficiency of your incident management process by setting SLOs and SLIs for incident response times, escalation efficiency, and communication effectiveness. This ensures that incidents are resolved promptly and that your response workflows are optimised.

By applying SLOs and SLIs to your observability stack, you gain valuable insights into the health and reliability of your monitoring tools. They serve as early warning systems, helping you identify and rectify issues before they impact your ability to effectively observe and manage your systems.

Hopefully you now have a comprehensive grasp of how alerting and anomaly detection amplify observability, and are now well-equipped to set up effective alerts, implement anomaly detection strategies, and manage incident response effectively. This knowledge empowers you and your team to maintain the health, performance, and reliability of their systems while minimising downtime and disruptions.

Chapter 8

Troubleshooting and Debugging

L et's start with a deep-dive into the art and science of troubleshooting and debugging using observability data. In this chapter I explore how observability tools and practices can be leveraged to identify, diagnose, and resolve issues within your software systems.

Troubleshooting

In the realm of software systems, troubleshooting stands as an indispensable pillar, holding up the edifice of reliability and functionality. This section will delve into the profound significance of troubleshooting, emphasising its pivotal role in maintaining the health and reliability of software systems. It underscores the importance of rapid issue identification and resolution to minimise user impact and system downtime.

8.1 The Need for Effective Troubleshooting

Software systems have become an integral part of our daily lives, powering everything from our smartphones to critical infrastructure. They are the digital engines that drive our world forward, but they are not impervious to glitches, bugs, and unforeseen issues. In this digital age, where the reliance on technology is pervasive, effective troubleshooting is more crucial than ever.

Troubleshooting is the process of identifying, diagnosing, and resolving problems within a software system. Its importance cannot be overstated, as it directly affects user satisfaction, productivity, and the bottom line of organisations. When software malfunctions or becomes unresponsive, it can lead to user frustration, lost revenue, and even security breaches.

One of the foremost reasons why troubleshooting is imperative is its role in minimising user impact. Imagine a scenario where a critical application used by a large number of employees in an organisation suddenly crashes. In such a situation, every minute of downtime translates into lost productivity and revenue. Effective troubleshooting can significantly reduce this downtime by swiftly identifying the root cause of the issue and implementing a solution.

Troubleshooting is a proactive measure that helps prevent minor issues from snowballing into catastrophic failures. By identifying and addressing problems early on, organisations can avoid costly and time-consuming system failures. In essence, troubleshooting acts as a preemptive safeguard, ensuring that software systems continue to operate smoothly.

In addition to minimising downtime and preventing major failures, effective troubleshooting is essential for maintaining the integrity and reliability of software systems. Over time, software can become vulnerable to various issues such as memory leaks, performance degradation, and compatibility problems. If left unattended, these issues can erode the overall quality of the software, leading to a decline in user satisfaction and trust.

Furthermore, the section highlights the fact that troubleshooting is not merely a reactive process. It is also a valuable tool for continuous improvement. By analysing the patterns of issues and their resolutions, organisations can identify areas for enhancement and refinement in their software systems. This data-driven approach can lead to better software design and development practices, ultimately resulting in more robust and reliable systems.

To underscore the critical role of troubleshooting, it is essential to recognise that the digital landscape is constantly evolving. New technologies, platforms, and software updates introduce fresh challenges and complexities. In such a dynamic environment, the ability to troubleshoot effectively becomes a strategic advantage. It empowers organisations to adapt to change, stay ahead of the competition, and deliver exceptional user experiences.

In conclusion, the need for effective troubleshooting in software systems cannot be overstated. It is a cornerstone of reliability, user satisfaction, and business success. Rapid issue identification and resolution not only minimise user impact and system downtime but also contribute to the continuous improvement of software systems. In an ever-changing digital landscape, mastering the art of troubleshooting is a skill that organisations and individuals alike must embrace to thrive in the world of technology.

8.2 Leveraging Observability Data for Troubleshooting

Here we are introduced to the concept of observability as a powerful ally in the troubleshooting process. We discuss how metrics, traces, and logs can provide valuable insights into the behaviour of applications and infrastructure components when issues arise.

Leveraging Observability Data for Troubleshooting: A Comprehensive Guide

In software systems, the ability to troubleshoot effectively is paramount. When issues arise in complex applications and infrastructure, pinpointing the root cause quickly becomes a critical task. To tackle this challenge, the concept of observability emerges as a powerful ally in the troubleshooting process. In this comprehensive guide, we will explore in depth how metrics, traces, and logs can provide invaluable insights into the behaviour of applications and infrastructure components when issues occur.

Let's recap, In previous chapters we learnt that Observability is the practice of gaining insights into the internal state of a system by examining its external outputs. It is a fundamental concept in modern software engineering and operations, enabling teams to understand, diagnose, and improve complex systems effectively.

At its core, observability revolves around three primary pillars:

1. Metrics: Metrics are quantitative measurements that provide continuous data about the performance and behaviour of a system. These can encompass a wide range of values, including CPU utilisation, memory usage, response times, error rates, and more. Metrics are collected and updated at regular intervals, providing a real-time view of system health.

2. Traces: Traces offer a way to trace the flow of requests or transactions as they move through a system. In distributed systems, where multiple services interact to process a single

request, it can be challenging to track down the source of issues. Traces, generated by instruments embedded in the code, allow for the visualisation of the complete journey of a request, showing which services it passed through and where delays or errors occurred.

3. Logs: Logs provide detailed textual records of events and activities within a system. These records capture not only errors but also contextual information surrounding events. Logs serve as a narrative of a system's behaviour, offering a chronological record of actions, errors, warnings, and other notable events.

This foundation helps us to understand **"The Power" of Metrics in Troubleshooting**

Metrics play a pivotal role in troubleshooting by providing quantitative data that offers a snapshot of a system's performance. Here are some specific scenarios where metrics prove indispensable:

1. Resource Utilisation Monitoring: Metrics such as CPU utilisation, memory usage, and disk I/O rates can reveal resource bottlenecks. For example, a sudden spike in CPU usage may indicate that a specific process or service is consuming an excessive amount of processing power, potentially causing performance degradation or outages.

2. Throughput and Response Times: Metrics related to request throughput and response times are vital for identifying performance issues. A drop in request throughput or a significant increase in response times can be early indicators of problems, such as network congestion or overloaded services.

3. Error Rate Analysis: Monitoring error rate metrics allows teams to quickly detect when the system is encountering errors. A sudden increase in error rates can signal issues like code bugs, misconfigurations, or external service disruptions, prompting immediate investigation.

4. Capacity Planning: Metrics data is essential for capacity planning. By analysing historical metrics, organisations can forecast future resource requirements, ensuring that the infrastructure can handle anticipated loads and preventing capacity-related issues.

Harnessing Traces for Troubleshooting

Traces offer a dynamic view of how requests traverse a system, making them invaluable for identifying bottlenecks and understanding complex interactions:

1. Identifying Latency Bottlenecks: In a microservices architecture, when users report slow response times, tracing becomes indispensable. A trace can visualise the entire journey of a request, showing which services it passed through and where delays occurred. Troubleshooters can identify the service responsible for the delay and focus their efforts on optimising it.

2. Transaction Error Isolation: Traces can be instrumental in isolating errors within transactions. For instance, if a user experiences an error during a multi-step transaction (e.g., a payment processing request), tracing can reveal which step of the transaction encountered the error. This allows teams to pinpoint the issue, whether it's a misconfiguration, a code bug, or an external dependency problem.

3. Service Dependency Mapping: In complex, interconnected systems, understanding dependencies is crucial. Traces can provide a visual representation of service dependencies, helping teams comprehend the intricate web of interactions and anticipate the impact of changes or failures in one service on the entire system.

Logs: A Treasure Trove of Troubleshooting Information

Logs are a rich source of data that offer a narrative of a system's behaviour. Here's how logs can be harnessed for troubleshooting:

1. Error Stack Tracing: When a software component encounters an error, logs provide a detailed account of what transpired leading up to the error. Stack traces within logs pinpoint the exact location in the code where the error occurred, streamlining the identification and resolution of bugs.

2. Security Incident Investigation: Logs are indispensable for investigating security incidents. Suspicious activities, unauthorised access attempts, and unusual login patterns often leave traces in logs. Security teams can analyse logs to trace back the sequence of events, understand the scope of a breach, and take immediate action to mitigate security risks.

3. Resource Exhaustion Detection: Logs can help identify resource exhaustion issues. For instance, when a database connection pool becomes exhausted, logs from the application layer can show a series of connection timeout errors. Analysing these logs can lead to the discovery of the issue and the adjustment of connection pool settings to prevent future problems.

4. Auditing and Compliance: Logs serve as a reliable record of system activities, which is critical for auditing and compliance purposes. In regulated industries, such as finance or healthcare, logs are often required to demonstrate adherence to security and data protection standards. Ok, so let's try and make some sense of all of this.

Putting It All Together: A Troubleshooting Scenario

To illustrate the synergy of metrics, traces, and logs in troubleshooting, let's consider a hypothetical scenario:

Scenario: A popular e-commerce website experiences a sudden increase in user complaints about slow checkout processes and, occasionally, orders failing to go through.

Using Metrics: The operations team starts by examining key metrics. They notice a significant spike in CPU utilisation and a rise in the error rate during the checkout process. These metrics indicate that resource constraints may be causing performance issues.

Using Traces: The development team decides to investigate further using traces. They trace a sample checkout transaction and discover that the process encounters a delay when communicating with the payment gateway service. The traces reveal a bottleneck in the payment processing step.

Using Logs: To uncover the root cause, the development team dives into the logs of the payment gateway service. In the logs, they find a recurring error related to a misconfigured API endpoint. This error is causing intermittent delays and occasional failures during payment processing.

Resolution: Armed with insights from metrics, traces, and logs, the teams quickly address the issue. They correct the misconfiguration in the payment gateway's API endpoint, leading to a significant improvement in checkout process performance.

This scenario demonstrates how the combined power of observability pillars—metrics, traces, and logs—enabled efficient troubleshooting and resolution of a complex issue. Metrics provided an initial indication of a problem, traces helped pinpoint the problematic step, and logs uncovered the specific misconfiguration causing the delay.

Proactive Observability: Beyond Troubleshooting

While observability is indispensable for troubleshooting, it also serves as a proactive approach to system health. Establishing robust observability practices can help organisations detect and address issues before they impact users. Here's how observability supports proactive measures:

1. Early Warning Signals: Anomalies in metrics, unusual traces, or warnings in logs can serve as early warning signals. For example, a

a gradual increase in memory usage or a consistent deviation from normal behaviour can indicate an impending issue. By setting up alerting mechanisms, teams can respond proactively to these signals.

2. Performance Optimisation: Continuous monitoring of metrics and traces allows organisations to identify opportunities for performance optimisation. By analysing the behaviour of applications and infrastructure over time, teams can make informed decisions about scaling, resource allocation, and code improvements.

3. Capacity Planning: Historical metrics data is invaluable for capacity planning. Organisations can use this data to predict resource requirements accurately and ensure that the infrastructure is prepared to handle anticipated loads, preventing capacity-related issues.

4. Quality Assurance: Observability is not limited to production environments. It can also be applied during the development and testing phases. Teams can use metrics, traces, and logs to monitor the behaviour of applications in staging and test environments, identifying and addressing issues before they reach production.

Observability through metrics, traces, and logs stands as a cornerstone of troubleshooting excellence in modern software systems. These observability pillars empower engineers, operators, and development teams to understand, diagnose, and resolve complex issues efficiently and effectively.

The power of observability lies not only in its ability to react to incidents but also in its capacity to proactively enhance system reliability and performance. By embracing observability as a core practice, organisations can ensure that their software systems remain resilient, responsive, and capable of delivering exceptional user experiences.

In the dynamic and ever-evolving landscape of technology, mastering observability is not just a best practice—it is a necessity for maintaining the health and reliability of software systems in an increasingly interconnected and complex world. As software systems continue to evolve, so too must our approaches to understanding and troubleshooting them, and observability provides the essential toolkit for doing just that.

8.3 Step-by-Step Troubleshooting Approach

The section outlines a systematic approach to troubleshooting, encompassing the following key steps:

1. Observation: How to effectively observe and monitor your systems using observability tools and dashboards.

2. Hypothesis Generation: Techniques for formulating hypotheses about the root cause of an issue based on observed data.

3. Experimentation: Conducting controlled experiments to validate or invalidate hypotheses and gather further data.

4. Root Cause Analysis: Techniques for identifying the underlying cause of the problem, whether it's related to code, infrastructure, or external factors.

5. Resolution and Documentation: Strategies for implementing fixes and documenting the troubleshooting process for future reference.

Title: A Systematic Approach to Troubleshooting: From Observation to Resolution

Effective troubleshooting is both an art and a science, and a systematic approach is key to swiftly and accurately resolving issues within complex systems. In this section, we will explore a step-by-step troubleshooting approach that encompasses the following key stages: Observation, Hypothesis Generation, Experimentation, Root Cause Analysis, and Resolution & Documentation.

1. Observation: Understanding the Current State

Observation is the first and arguably the most critical step in the troubleshooting process. It involves effectively observing and monitoring your systems using observability tools and dashboards. Here are key aspects of this phase:

- Monitoring Tools: Utilise monitoring and observability tools to keep a watchful eye on system metrics, traces, and logs. These tools provide real-time data on the health and performance of your applications and infrastructure.

- Alerting Systems: Set up alerting systems to notify you when specific thresholds are exceeded or anomalies are detected. This allows you to proactively address potential issues before they impact users.

- Baseline Understanding: Establish a baseline understanding of what "normal" behaviour looks like for your system. This baseline serves as a reference point for identifying deviations that may indicate problems.

2. Hypothesis Generation: Formulating Educated Guesses

Once you've gathered observational data, the next step is to formulate hypotheses about the root cause of the issue based on that data. Hypothesis generation involves using your knowledge of the system to make educated guesses about what might be causing the problem:

- Pattern Recognition: Look for patterns and correlations in your data. For instance, if you observe a sudden spike in error rates coinciding with a code deployment, you might hypothesise that the new code is causing the issue.

- Ask Questions: Formulate questions about the observed behaviour. For example, "Could this slow response time be due to a database bottleneck?" These questions can guide your hypotheses.

- Prioritise Hypotheses: Rank your hypotheses based on likelihood and potential impact. Start with the most probable causes to expedite the troubleshooting process.

3. Experimentation: Testing Your Hypotheses

Experimentation involves conducting controlled experiments to validate or invalidate your hypotheses and gather further data. Here's how to approach this phase:

- Isolate Variables: In your experiments, isolate variables to pinpoint the cause-effect relationship. For example, if you suspect a database issue, conduct tests with and without database queries to see if there's a correlation.

- Collect Data: Carefully collect data during your experiments. This data can include metrics, traces, and logs that provide evidence for or against your hypotheses.

- Document Changes: Make systematic changes to the system based on your hypotheses, and document these changes. This documentation ensures that you can easily roll back changes if they do not yield the expected results.

4. Root Cause Analysis: Identifying the Underlying Cause

Root Cause Analysis is the heart of troubleshooting, where you identify the underlying cause of the problem. Techniques for this phase include:

- Correlation Analysis: Analyse the data collected during experimentation to correlate changes or anomalies with the occurrence of the issue. This correlation can lead you closer to the root cause.

- Impact Analysis: Consider the broader impact of the issue. Does it affect a single component, or does it have cascading effects on other parts of the system? Understanding the scope of the problem is essential for accurate root cause identification.

- External Factors: Don't overlook external factors. Sometimes, issues are caused by changes in third-party services, network conditions, or external dependencies.

5. Resolution and Documentation: Fixing the Problem and Learning for the Future

Once the root cause is identified, it's time to implement fixes and document the troubleshooting process for future reference:

- Resolution: Implement the necessary fixes to address the root cause of the issue. Ensure that these changes are thoroughly tested to prevent unintended consequences.

- Documentation: Document the entire troubleshooting process, including observations, hypotheses, experiments, and the final resolution. This documentation serves as a valuable resource for future troubleshooting efforts and knowledge sharing within your team.

- Knowledge Sharing: Share your findings and learnings with your team. Troubleshooting is not just about solving immediate issues but also about building collective knowledge to prevent similar problems in the future.

In conclusion, a systematic approach to troubleshooting, encompassing Observation, Hypothesis Generation, Experimentation, Root Cause Analysis, and Resolution & Documentation, is essential for effectively resolving issues within complex systems. By following these steps, you can streamline the troubleshooting process, minimise downtime, and build a repository of knowledge to enhance your team's troubleshooting capabilities over time. Troubleshooting is not just about solving immediate problems; it's about learning and improving to create more resilient systems.

8.4 Real-World Troubleshooting Scenarios

The section provides real-world troubleshooting scenarios to illustrate how observability data can be applied in practice. These scenarios cover a range of common issues, from performance bottlenecks to errors in microservices architectures.

Real-World Troubleshooting Scenarios: Harnessing Observability Data

Troubleshooting is a multifaceted practice, and the ability to apply observability data in real-world scenarios is crucial for IT professionals across various roles. In this section, we will explore a series of real-world troubleshooting scenarios that span a spectrum of common issues. These scenarios will showcase how observability data can be effectively leveraged in practice, highlighting the contributions of different IT roles within each example.

Scenario 1: Performance Bottleneck in an E-commerce Application

Roles: Operations Engineer, DevOps Engineer, Software Developer

Problem Description: A popular e-commerce application experiences slow response times during peak shopping hours, leading to frustrated customers and lost sales.

Observation: Operations engineers, armed with observability tools and dashboards, observe a significant increase in CPU utilisation and a spike in error rates during peak hours.

Hypothesis Generation: DevOps engineers hypothesise that

the increase in traffic during peak hours is causing resource contention, leading to high CPU usage and errors.

Experimentation: DevOps engineers conduct controlled experiments, scaling up the application servers to handle increased load. They monitor metrics in real-time to assess the impact of the changes.

Root Cause Analysis: Post-experiment, DevOps engineers analyse the data and discover that scaling up the application servers mitigated the performance issues. The root cause is identified as inadequate server capacity during peak hours.

Resolution and Documentation: DevOps engineers provision additional servers and implement auto-scaling policies to dynamically adjust resources during traffic spikes. The entire troubleshooting process, including observations, experiments, and solutions, is documented for future reference.

Scenario 2: Database Slowdown in a Finance Application

Roles: Database Administrator (DBA), Software Developer

Problem Description: A finance application experiences frequent database slowdowns, impacting critical financial transactions.

Observation: Database administrators monitor database performance metrics and notice a sustained increase in query execution times during peak business hours.

Hypothesis Generation: DBAs hypothesise that poorly optimised SQL queries may be responsible for the slowdown, causing resource contention on the database server.

Experimentation: Software developers collaborate with DBAs to identify and optimise resource-intensive SQL queries. They deploy query optimisations to a test environment and monitor the impact on query performance.

Root Cause Analysis: Post-optimisation, DBAs and developers observe significant improvements in query execution times. The root cause is traced back to inefficient SQL queries.

Resolution and Documentation: Developers implement the optimised SQL queries in the production environment, resulting in improved database performance. DBAs document the query optimisation process for future reference and performance tuning.

Scenario 3: Microservices Communication Error

Roles: DevOps Engineer, Software Developer

Problem Description: An organisation's microservices architecture encounters intermittent communication errors, disrupting critical data flow between services.

Observation: DevOps engineers utilise tracing tools to visualise request flows and identify that communication errors tend to occur when a specific microservice is involved.

Hypothesis Generation: DevOps engineers hypothesise that the microservice responsible for the communication error may experience intermittent downtime or latency issues.

Experimentation: DevOps engineers and software developers collaborate to conduct controlled experiments. They introduce retries and circuit breakers in the affected microservice to handle intermittent communication issues more gracefully.

Root Cause Analysis: After implementing retry mechanisms, the communication errors are significantly reduced. The root cause is attributed to occasional latency in the microservice under scrutiny.

Resolution and Documentation: Developers optimise the microservice to reduce latency, and DevOps engineers implement improved monitoring and alerting for communication errors. The entire troubleshooting process, including observations, experiments, and solutions, is documented for future microservices-related incidents.

Scenario 4: Network Latency in a Distributed System

Roles: Network Engineer, DevOps Engineer, Software Developer

Problem Description: A distributed system experiences unexplained network latency, leading to increased request times between services.

Observation: Network engineers use network monitoring tools to detect network latency spikes and identify specific network segments where latency is consistently higher.

Hypothesis Generation: Network engineers collaborate with DevOps engineers and software developers to hypothesise that the high network latency may be caused by congestion or misconfigured network equipment.

Experimentation: DevOps engineers conduct network traffic analysis experiments, rerouting traffic through alternative network paths to evaluate the impact on latency.

Root Cause Analysis: Post-experiments, it is determined that rerouting traffic improved latency, suggesting that specific network segments were experiencing congestion. The root cause is attributed to network congestion.

Resolution and Documentation: Network engineers optimise network routes, implement Quality of Service (QoS) policies, and configure monitoring to proactively detect and address network congestion. The entire troubleshooting process, including observations, experiments, and network optimisations, is documented for future reference.

Scenario 5: Application Security Breach

Roles: Security Analyst, Software Developer

Problem Description: An organisation suspects a security breach as unauthorised access attempts and unusual activities are detected in their web application.

Observation: Security analysts review security logs and notice a series of suspicious login attempts, unusual access patterns, and unexpected data transfers.

Hypothesis Generation: Security analysts hypothesise that the security breach may be due to weak authentication mechanisms or vulnerabilities in the application code.

Experimentation: Software developers collaborate with security analysts to conduct vulnerability assessments and penetration testing on the application. They simulate attack scenarios to identify potential vulnerabilities.

Root Cause Analysis: Vulnerability assessments reveal several security vulnerabilities, including weak authentication mechanisms. The root cause is identified as a combination of code vulnerabilities and weak security practices.

Resolution and Documentation: Software developers implement security patches, strengthen authentication mechanisms, and establish rigorous security practices. Security analysts document the breach detection and resolution process, sharing insights and lessons learned to enhance the organisation's security posture.

In these real-world troubleshooting scenarios, different IT roles collaborate to effectively leverage observability data. Whether it's resolving performance bottlenecks, optimising database queries, addressing microservices communication errors, mitigating network latency, or responding to security breaches, observability tools and data play a pivotal role in identifying root causes and implementing solutions. Troubleshooting, in practice, is a collaborative effort that draws upon the expertise of multiple IT professionals, each contributing their skills to restore system health and enhance overall resilience.

8.5 Debugging in Production

Debugging in production can be challenging but is sometimes necessary. The section explores best practices for safe debugging in production environments, ensuring minimal disruption to users while diagnosing and resolving issues.

Debugging in a production environment can indeed be a high-stakes and delicate endeavour. When an issue occurs in a live system, it may not always be feasible to replicate the problem in a controlled testing environment. However, with the right approach and best practices, you can minimise disruptions to users while effectively diagnosing and resolving issues. Here's some advice for safe debugging in production:

1. Prioritise Safety and Minimise Risk:
   - Assess the Impact: Before you start debugging in production, evaluate the potential risks and impact of your actions. Consider the criticality of the issue and the potential consequences of debugging. Ensure that your actions won't disrupt essential services or compromise data integrity.

   - Use Staging or Canary Environments: Whenever possible, use a staging or canary environment to replicate the production setup. This allows you to test your debugging procedures in a controlled environment before applying them in the live production environment.

2. Implement Comprehensive Monitoring:

   - Instrument Your Code: Incorporate extensive monitoring and observability practices into your code and infrastructure.

This includes setting up metrics, traces, and logs that provide real-time insights into system behaviour. A well-instrumented system makes it easier to pinpoint issues when they occur.

- Alerting and Thresholds: Configure alerting systems to notify you when key metrics deviate from expected norms. Establish thresholds for alerting so that you can proactively respond to potential issues before they become critical.

3. Isolate Debugging Environments:
- Sandbox Environments: Whenever possible, use sandbox or isolated environments for debugging. These environments should closely resemble the production setup but are separate from it, reducing the risk of accidental disruptions.

- Feature Flags: Implement feature flags or toggles in your code. These allow you to enable or disable specific features or code paths without deploying new code, providing a level of control and isolation during debugging.

4. Use Read-Only and Non-Destructive Actions:

- Avoid Write Operations: When debugging in production, refrain from making write operations or modifications that could alter data or system state. Instead, focus on inspecting and gathering information.

- Dry Runs: If possible, perform dry runs of debugging procedures to validate their safety before executing them on the live system. This is particularly important for complex or high-risk debugging tasks.

5. Leverage Observability Data:

- Metrics, Traces, and Logs: Rely heavily on observability data, such as metrics, traces, and logs. Use these data sources to identify the affected components and narrow down potential causes before taking action.

- Analyse Patterns: Examine historical observability data to identify patterns or trends related to the issue. This data can guide your debugging efforts and help you make informed decisions.

6. Limit Debugging Access:

- Role-Based Access Control (RBAC): Implement RBAC to restrict access to debugging tools and environments. Ensure that only authorised personnel have access to debugging resources.

- Temporary Access: Grant temporary access rights or permissions for debugging purposes, and revoke them once the debugging is complete. This reduces the risk of unauthorised access or accidental changes.

7. Communicate Transparently:

- Notify Stakeholders: If debugging activities have the potential to impact users or services, communicate transparently with relevant stakeholders, such as customers or internal teams. Provide clear information about the nature of the issue, your debugging plan, and expected timelines for resolution.

- Change Logs: Maintain detailed change logs of all actions taken during the debugging process. This documentation serves as an audit trail and can be invaluable for post-debugging analysis and reporting.

8. Prepare Rollback Procedures:

- Rollback Plans: Always have a rollback plan in place in case your debugging efforts inadvertently worsen the situation or introduce new issues. Ensure that you can revert to a known good state quickly.

9. Monitor Continuously:

- Real-Time Monitoring: Continuously monitor the system as you debug to assess the impact of your actions in real-time. Be ready to react promptly if unexpected issues arise during debugging.

10. Post-Mortem Analysis:

- Learn from the Experience: After the debugging process is complete and the issue is resolved, conduct a post-mortem analysis. Document the root cause, actions taken, and lessons learned. Use this information to improve future debugging processes and prevent similar issues.

By following these best practices, you can engage in safe debugging in production environments, ensuring that you address issues while minimising the risk of disruption. Remember that each situation is unique, and it's crucial to exercise caution and prioritise the stability and reliability of your systems throughout the debugging process.

8.6 Collaboration and Knowledge Sharing

Effective troubleshooting often involves collaboration among team members. We discuss strategies for fostering a culture of knowledge sharing and collaboration, ensuring that insights gained during troubleshooting are disseminated across the organisation.

Collaboration and knowledge sharing are indispensable components of effective troubleshooting within any organisation. When tackling complex issues, a collective effort and the dissemination of insights are key to swift and lasting resolutions.

Fostering a culture of collaboration starts with encouraging open communication among team members. This can be achieved through regular meetings, brainstorming sessions, and collaborative tools that facilitate real-time information sharing. Cross-functional teams, involving members from different IT roles, can bring diverse perspectives to the troubleshooting process, leading to more comprehensive solutions.

Knowledge sharing should be a continuous practice. Documenting troubleshooting processes, solutions, and lessons learned ensures that valuable insights are not lost. Centralised knowledge repositories, wikis, or documentation platforms can serve as accessible resources for all team members. Additionally, instituting post-incident reviews or retrospectives allows teams to reflect on past troubleshooting experiences, identify areas for improvement, and collectively learn from their successes and challenges.

Ultimately, a culture of collaboration and knowledge sharing transforms troubleshooting from an isolated activity into a collective and dynamic endeavour, empowering teams to resolve issues more effectively while building a reservoir of expertise that benefits the entire organisation.

By the end of the chapter, you should now have a comprehensive understanding of how to harness observability data for effective troubleshooting and debugging. Equipped with a systematic approach to problem-solving, enabling you to tackle issues efficiently and minimise their impact on users and business operations. Troubleshooting becomes not just a reactive process but an opportunity for continuous improvement and system resilience.

Chapter 9

Scalability and Performance Optimisation

C hapter 9, delves into the critical realm of scalability and performance optimisation through the lens of observability. This chapter explores how observability practices can be instrumental in identifying bottlenecks, optimising resource usage, and ensuring your systems scale effectively to meet increasing demands.

9.1 The Imperative of Scalability

The chapter begins by emphasising the fundamental importance of scalability in modern software systems. Scalability ensures that your applications can handle growing workloads without compromising performance or user experience. We explore the various dimensions of scalability, from vertical scaling to horizontal scaling, and why each is relevant in different contexts.

Scale Resources

The Imperative of Scalability

In modern software systems, one concept stands out as an imperative that can make or break the success of an application: scalability. This section delves into the fundamental importance of scalability, highlighting its role in ensuring that software applications can handle increasing workloads while maintaining peak performance and an optimal user experience. Scalability isn't merely an option; it's a critical necessity in the world of software development.

At its core, scalability is about an application's ability to grow and adapt in response to changing demands. This ability can be visualised through two primary dimensions: vertical scaling and horizontal scaling, each carrying its own significance and relevance in various contexts.

Vertical scaling involves enhancing the capabilities of a single machine, such as adding more CPU cores, memory, or storage capacity. This approach can temporarily boost an application's performance, making it a valuable solution for certain scenarios. However, it has limitations, as there's a practical limit to how much a single machine can be upgraded. Once that limit is reached, vertical scaling can become prohibitively expensive and may still not provide the desired level of scalability for extremely high-demand applications.

This is where horizontal scaling comes into play. Unlike vertical scaling, which focuses on a single machine's capabilities, horizontal scaling is about distributing the load across multiple machines or instances. This approach provides a more sustainable and cost-effective way to achieve scalability. As the workload increases, additional machines can be added to the cluster, allowing the application to handle higher traffic volumes seamlessly. Horizontal scaling, often associated with cloud computing and containerisation technologies, has become the cornerstone of modern software architecture.

The relevance of vertical and horizontal scaling varies based on the specific requirements of an application. For instance, an e-commerce website might initially rely on vertical scaling to meet the demands of a growing user base. However, as traffic continues to surge, the cost and complexity of vertical scaling may become unsustainable. In such cases, transitioning to horizontal scaling becomes essential, ensuring that the application can handle not only more users but also maintain a consistent level of performance.

Scalability also extends beyond the technical realm; it has a profound impact on business strategies and competitiveness. In today's fast-paced digital environment, user expectations are at an all-time high. Users demand not only fast and reliable services but also the ability to access those services at any time and from any device. Failure to deliver on these expectations can result in user attrition, lost revenue, and damage to the brand's reputation.

Furthermore, scalability plays a pivotal role in cost management. Inefficiently scaled applications can lead to over-provisioning, where resources are underutilised, or under-provisioning, where resources are overwhelmed. Both scenarios result in wasted expenditure or missed opportunities. Properly scaling an application, however, ensures that resources are allocated optimally, striking a balance between performance and cost-effectiveness.

The Imperative of Scalability, therefore, transcends the boundaries of technology, extending its reach into the realms of user satisfaction, financial prudence, and competitiveness. In a world where digital services are central to almost every aspect of daily life, scalable software systems are the backbone of success. Embracing both vertical and horizontal scaling strategies allows organisations to not only meet the current demands but also remain adaptable to the ever-evolving landscape of technology.

In conclusion, scalability is not an optional feature in modern software systems; it is a fundamental imperative. It empowers applications to grow and adapt to changing workloads, ensuring optimal performance and user satisfaction. Vertical scaling and horizontal scaling are the twin pillars of scalability, each with its own relevance in different contexts. As businesses navigate the digital age, understanding and implementing scalability strategies is essential to thrive in a world where the only constant is change.

9.2 Monitoring for Scalability

Effective scalability hinges on a deep understanding of your system's behaviour under various load conditions. This section outlines how observability tools and practices enable you to monitor key performance indicators (KPIs) and gather data that reveals the scalability of your applications and infrastructure.

Monitoring for Scalability: The Path to Sustainable Growth

The pursuit of scalability is a perpetual journey. As the demands on digital systems continue to evolve, organisations must equip themselves with the tools and practices necessary to ensure their applications and infrastructure can grow in tandem. At the heart of this endeavour lies the crucial section of monitoring for scalability. Effective scalability necessitates not only the ability to scale up but also the insight to understand precisely when and how to do so. This section explores the significance of observability tools and practices in achieving scalability by closely monitoring key performance indicators (KPIs) and gathering data that illuminates the system's scalability under various load conditions.

At its essence, scalability is the capacity of a system to handle increased workloads efficiently and without compromising performance. Achieving scalability requires a comprehensive understanding of how your application behaves as load fluctuates. To achieve this understanding, observability becomes indispensable. Observability encompasses the tools, practices, and culture that enable organisations to gain insights into the inner workings of their systems.

Observability tools, such as application performance monitoring (APM) systems, log analysers, and infrastructure monitoring platforms, allow teams to keep a watchful eye on crucial KPIs. These KPIs vary depending on the system but often include metrics like response times, error rates, and resource utilisation. By continuously collecting and analysing these metrics, teams can detect performance bottlenecks, identify areas for optimisation, and gauge how the system responds to increased loads.

One of the primary advantages of observability tools is their ability to provide real-time insights. In today's fast-paced digital landscape, the ability to identify and respond to performance issues as they occur is paramount. Real-time monitoring allows teams to proactively address scalability challenges before they spiral into crises, ensuring a seamless user experience even during periods of high demand.

Another critical aspect of monitoring for scalability is load testing. Load testing involves simulating high levels of traffic or load on a system to understand how it performs under stress. By conducting load tests, organisations can pinpoint the breaking points of their applications and infrastructure. This information is invaluable for making informed decisions about when and how to scale up.

Monitoring for scalability is not a one-time endeavour but an ongoing practice. As applications and workloads evolve, so too must monitoring strategies. Scalability is not a one-size-fits-all concept; it is highly contextual. What works for one application may not be suitable for another. Therefore, the ability to adapt and fine-tune monitoring practices is essential.

Additionally, observability practices should be integrated into the broader DevOps culture of an organisation. Collaboration between development and operations teams, along with a shared commitment to monitoring and improving system performance, is crucial. A DevOps approach ensures that scalability is not an afterthought but an integral part of the development and deployment process.

This section on monitoring for scalability is a pivotal element in the journey toward building robust and adaptable software systems. It underscores the significance of observability tools and practices in monitoring KPIs and gathering essential data. By continuously assessing how a system performs under various load conditions and being prepared to scale up when needed, organisations can not only meet current demands but also position themselves for sustainable growth in an ever-changing digital landscape. Monitoring for scalability is not a luxury; it is a necessity for those who seek to thrive in a world where scalability is the key to resilience and success.

9.3 Identifying Performance Bottlenecks

Let's look at how to use observability data to identify performance bottlenecks. We will explore techniques for pinpointing issues related to CPU, memory, disk I/O, network latency, and more. This knowledge empowers teams to address performance bottlenecks proactively, ensuring optimal system responsiveness.

Identifying Performance Bottlenecks: A Guide to Utilising Observability Data

In the fast-paced world of software development, optimal system performance is the holy grail. Users expect applications to be lightning-fast, responsive, and capable of handling ever-increasing workloads. However, achieving and maintaining this level of performance is no small feat. It requires the ability to identify and mitigate performance bottlenecks effectively. In this comprehensive guide, we will explore how to use observability data to pinpoint issues related to CPU, memory, disk I/O, network latency, and more. Armed with this knowledge, teams can proactively address performance bottlenecks, ensuring that their systems remain responsive and reliable.

Performance bottlenecks are points in a system where the throughput or responsiveness is limited or constrained, often due to resource limitations. Identifying these bottlenecks is a critical step in optimising system performance. Observability data, which encompasses metrics, logs, and traces, provides valuable insights into system behaviour. By closely monitoring key performance indicators (KPIs) and using the right tools, teams can uncover the root causes of bottlenecks and take appropriate actions.

Let's delve into some common performance bottlenecks and the techniques for identifying them:

1. CPU Bottlenecks:

Symptoms: High CPU utilisation, increased response times, and system slowdowns.

Identification Techniques: Utilise CPU metrics to monitor

overall utilisation and identify processes or threads that consume excessive CPU resources. Profiling tools can help pinpoint specific functions or code segments causing CPU spikes. For example, in a web application, you might use profiling tools like `perf` or built-in profiler tools provided by programming languages like Python's `cProfile` or Java's `VisualVM`.

2. Memory Bottlenecks:

Symptoms: Frequent garbage collection (in languages with garbage collection), high memory usage, and application crashes due to out-of-memory errors.

Identification Techniques: Monitor memory-related metrics such as heap usage, garbage collection frequency, and memory leaks. Tools like heap profilers (e.g., Java's VisualVM or .NET's CLR Profiler) can help identify memory-hungry components. Additionally, analysing memory dumps or using memory profilers like Valgrind can uncover memory leaks and inefficient memory usage.

3. Disk I/O Bottlenecks:

Symptoms: Slow disk read/write operations, high disk queue lengths, and prolonged response times.

Identification Techniques: Track disk I/O metrics, including disk read/write rates and latency. Identify processes or files generating excessive disk I/O. Tools like `iostat` on Unix-based systems can provide valuable insights into disk activity. Additionally, profiling file access patterns within the application can reveal inefficient disk usage.

4. Network Latency Bottlenecks:

Symptoms: High network latency, slow data transfer, and delayed responses.

Identification Techniques: Monitor network-related metrics,

such as network latency, packet loss, and bandwidth utilisation. Tracing tools like Wireshark can help diagnose network issues by capturing and analysing network packets. Profiling network communication within the application can also highlight bottlenecks, such as inefficient API calls or database queries.

5. Concurrency Bottlenecks:

Symptoms: Poor scalability, contention for shared resources, and thread/process bottlenecks.

Identification Techniques: Employ concurrency profiling and monitoring tools to identify contention points. For instance, Java applications can use tools like Thread Dump Analyser (TDA) to analyse thread dumps and pinpoint threads stuck in locks. Profiling concurrent code paths using thread profilers can reveal bottlenecks related to synchronisation.

6. Database Bottlenecks:

Symptoms: Slow database queries, high database load, and database connection pool exhaustion.

Identification Techniques: Monitor database-related metrics, such as query execution time, database load, and connection pool usage. Database query profiling tools like `EXPLAIN` in SQL databases or database-specific query analysers can help optimise slow queries. Examining database logs can provide insights into slow or blocked queries.

7. Application Code Bottlenecks:

Symptoms: Slow response times, inefficient algorithms, and suboptimal code.

Identification Techniques: Profiling tools and performance monitoring can pinpoint bottlenecks within the application code. For example, in a Python application, you can use cProfile or more specialised profilers like `line_profiler` to identify slow functions or lines of code. Optimisation tools like Valgrind or

Google's `perf` can analyse code execution at a low level.

8. Third-party Service Bottlenecks:

Symptoms: Delays caused by external services or dependencies.

Identification Techniques: Monitoring external service response times and error rates is crucial. Tools like distributed tracing (e.g., OpenTelemetry or Zipkin) can help trace requests across multiple services and pinpoint bottlenecks in third-party interactions. Additionally, using circuit breakers and retries can mitigate issues caused by unreliable external services.

9. Infrastructure Bottlenecks:

Symptoms: Resource exhaustion due to inadequate infrastructure provisioning.

Identification Techniques: Monitoring infrastructure metrics such as CPU, memory, and disk usage can reveal resource constraints. Auto-scaling and infrastructure as code (IaC) practices can help dynamically provision resources to meet demand and prevent infrastructure-related bottlenecks.

In practice, a combination of monitoring tools, profiling, and log analysis is often necessary to identify and resolve performance bottlenecks comprehensively. Moreover, it's important to establish a proactive performance optimisation workflow that includes regular performance testing and tuning to address bottlenecks as they arise.

To illustrate these concepts with an example, consider a popular e-commerce website experiencing slow page load times during peak shopping seasons. By monitoring CPU, memory, and database query execution times, the operations team notices spikes in CPU utilisation and extended query execution times during high traffic periods. Profiling the application code reveals inefficient database queries that could be optimised. By optimising these queries and implementing database connection pooling, the team successfully mitigates the performance bottleneck, resulting in faster page load times and a better user experience.

In conclusion, identifying performance bottlenecks is a fundamental aspect of maintaining optimal system responsiveness. Utilising observability data, teams can pinpoint issues related to CPU, memory, disk I/O, network latency, and more. By employing the appropriate monitoring tools and profiling techniques, organisations can proactively address bottlenecks, ensuring that their systems remain reliable and performant even in the face of increasing workloads. Remember, performance optimisation is an ongoing process, and staying vigilant is key to delivering exceptional user experiences.

9.4 Capacity Planning and Resource Allocation

Capacity planning is crucial for anticipating resource needs as your systems scale. The section discusses strategies for capacity planning and resource allocation, leveraging observability data to make informed decisions about scaling your infrastructure horizontally or vertically.

Capacity Planning and Resource Allocation: Scaling with Confidence

As digital systems continue to evolve, one of the pivotal aspects of ensuring their stability and performance is effective capacity planning and resource allocation. This section delves into the strategies and principles behind capacity planning and resource allocation, highlighting the importance of utilising observability data to make informed decisions about scaling infrastructure horizontally or vertically. In a world where the demands on digital systems are ever-increasing, the ability to anticipate resource needs and allocate them judiciously is critical.

Capacity planning is a proactive approach to forecasting and preparing for future resource requirements. It is an essential practice to prevent system overloads, downtimes, and degraded performance as your applications and user base grow. Successful capacity planning involves several key steps:

1. Data Collection and Analysis: Observability tools, which encompass monitoring, logging, and tracing, provide valuable insights into system behaviour. Data collected from these tools helps identify performance bottlenecks, resource utilisation patterns, and growth trends. For example, monitoring tools can reveal that CPU utilisation consistently reaches 90% during peak hours, indicating a need for additional CPU resources.

2. Benchmarking and Performance Testing: Conducting performance tests under varying load conditions helps determine system limits and bottlenecks. Benchmarking provides a baseline for resource utilisation and response times, aiding in capacity planning. Performance tests can simulate future workloads and assess system behaviour under those conditions.

3. Scalability Analysis: Understanding the scalability characteristics of your applications and infrastructure is crucial. Vertical scaling involves adding more resources to existing components (e.g., increasing CPU or memory), while horizontal scaling entails adding more instances of components. Evaluating which scaling strategy aligns with your system's requirements is essential for effective capacity planning.

4. Forecasting: Based on historical data, performance testing results, and scalability analysis, create forecasts for future resource needs. Consider factors like user growth, seasonal variations, and application feature changes. A well-informed

forecast can guide resource allocation decisions.

5. Resource Allocation: Decide how to allocate resources, whether by upgrading existing hardware (vertical scaling) or adding more instances (horizontal scaling). Resource allocation should be based on the forecasted needs while allowing room for flexibility to adapt to unexpected spikes in demand.

6. Monitoring and Iteration: After resource allocation, continue to monitor the system's performance. Adjust capacity plans as needed based on real-world data and user feedback. Capacity planning is not a one-time task; it requires ongoing refinement.

Resource allocation is the practical implementation of capacity planning. It involves distributing resources, such as CPU, memory, storage, and network capacity, to meet the forecasted demand effectively. Here are some strategies for resource allocation:

1. Vertical Scaling: This approach involves adding more resources to existing hardware or virtual machines. For example, upgrading a server's CPU or memory can address increased demand. Vertical scaling is suitable when you have room to expand your current infrastructure and want to make the most of your existing investments.

2. Horizontal Scaling: Horizontal scaling entails adding more instances of a component or service to distribute the workload. It is a more flexible approach and is commonly used in cloud-based environments. For instance, if a web application experiences higher traffic, adding more web servers can distribute the load efficiently.

3. Auto-scaling: Leveraging auto-scaling mechanisms allows infrastructure to adapt dynamically to changing demands. Cloud providers offer auto-scaling solutions that can automatically add or remove instances based on predefined conditions, such as CPU utilisation or network traffic.

4. Resource Pools: Resource pools allocate a fixed amount of resources to different components or services within an infrastructure. Each component has access to its dedicated resource pool, ensuring that one component's resource usage does not negatively impact others.

5. Load Balancing: Load balancers distribute incoming traffic across multiple servers or instances, ensuring even resource utilisation and fault tolerance. Load balancing is a critical component of horizontally scalable architectures.

Let's illustrate these concepts with an example: Consider an e-commerce platform preparing for the holiday season, which historically experiences a significant increase in traffic. Based on past data and performance testing, the capacity planning team forecasts a 30% increase in user traffic during the holiday period. To accommodate this surge, they opt for horizontal scaling by adding more web server instances behind a load balancer. Additionally, they configure auto-scaling rules to dynamically adjust the number of instances based on CPU utilisation.

Capacity planning and resource allocation are not one-size-fits-all endeavours; they require tailored strategies that align with your organisation's specific needs and infrastructure. The ability to leverage observability data to make informed decisions about scaling, whether horizontally or vertically, empowers organisations to confidently meet growing demands while maintaining system stability and performance. In a digital landscape where scalability is synonymous with competitiveness, effective capacity planning and resource allocation are strategic imperatives.

9.5 Load Testing and Chaos Engineering

To validate scalability and resilience, load testing and chaos engineering are indispensable practices. The section introduces you to these concepts and explains how observability plays a pivotal role in designing, executing, and analysing the results of such tests.

Load Testing and Chaos Engineering: Fortifying Scalability and Resilience

In the relentless pursuit of robust and resilient software systems, two indispensable practices come to the forefront: load testing and chaos engineering. This section introduces you to these concepts and elucidates their crucial role in ensuring scalability and resilience. Furthermore, it underscores the pivotal role of observability in the design, execution, and analysis of load tests and chaos experiments, guiding organisations toward more reliable and adaptable digital infrastructures.

Load Testing: Ensuring Scalability

Load testing is a systematic process of subjecting a software application or system to simulated workloads to evaluate its performance under different levels of stress. The primary goal is to assess scalability, i.e., how well the system can handle varying degrees of load without compromising performance or stability. Load testing helps organisations identify bottlenecks, resource limitations, and other performance issues before they impact users.

Load tests involve the following key steps:

1. Test Scenario Definition: Determine the use cases, traffic patterns, and workloads that your application is likely to face in real-world scenarios. For instance, an e-commerce website might simulate concurrent user sessions, each performing actions like browsing, searching, and making purchases.

2. Load Generation: Use load testing tools to simulate user interactions and generate artificial traffic to the application.

These tools can simulate hundreds or thousands of concurrent users, allowing you to assess how the system behaves under different levels of load.

3. Performance Metrics: Define key performance indicators (KPIs) that align with your application's goals, such as response times, error rates, and throughput. These metrics serve as benchmarks to evaluate the system's performance.

4. Execution and Monitoring: Run the load tests while closely monitoring the system's behaviour using observability tools. These tools provide real-time data on metrics like response times, resource utilisation, and error rates.

5. Analysis and Optimisation: After completing the tests, analyse the results to identify performance bottlenecks or areas for improvement. Adjust the application, infrastructure, or configuration to optimise performance based on the findings.

Load testing is a proactive practice that helps organisations anticipate and address performance issues before they impact end-users. It enables them to fine-tune their systems for optimal scalability, ensuring that as user traffic grows, the application remains responsive and reliable.

Chaos Engineering: Building Resilience Through Controlled Chaos

Chaos engineering is an engineering discipline that involves intentionally injecting controlled failures and chaos into a system to assess its resilience and ability to withstand unexpected disruptions. Rather than aiming to identify performance bottlenecks, chaos engineering focuses on uncovering vulnerabilities that can lead to system failures.

Chaos experiments involve the following principles:

1. Hypothesis Creation: Formulate hypotheses about potential weaknesses or vulnerabilities within your system. For example,

you might hypothesise that a sudden increase in traffic will cause the system to fail.

2. Experiment Design: Design controlled experiments to test these hypotheses. Introduce disruptions, such as network latency, server failures, or database outages, into the system to see how it responds.

3. Execution and Monitoring: Execute the chaos experiments while continuously monitoring the system's behaviour. Observability tools play a critical role in tracking the impact of chaos on performance, identifying unexpected consequences, and ensuring the system returns to a stable state.

4. Analysis and Remediation: Analyse the results of the chaos experiments to validate or invalidate the initial hypotheses. If vulnerabilities are identified, take remedial actions to improve system resilience. This may involve redesigning the architecture, implementing failover mechanisms, or enhancing error handling.

Chaos engineering aims to create systems that are more resilient to failures and disruptions. By intentionally introducing controlled chaos, organisations can uncover weaknesses in their infrastructure, applications, and processes, leading to proactive improvements that enhance overall system reliability.

The Role of Observability

Observability is a cornerstone of both load testing and chaos engineering. It provides the visibility and data needed to design, execute, and analyse the results of these tests effectively. Observability tools offer real-time insights into system behaviour, allowing organisations to:

- Monitor the impact of increased load during load testing.
- Track performance metrics and resource utilisation during chaos experiments.
- Identify unexpected behaviour or vulnerabilities that may

arise during testing.
- Analyse the results to fine-tune the system for improved scalability and resilience.

In conclusion, load testing and chaos engineering are indispensable practices for organisations seeking to fortify the scalability and resilience of their digital systems. These practices enable proactive identification and resolution of performance bottlenecks and vulnerabilities. Observability, through monitoring, logging, and tracing, plays a pivotal role in facilitating these tests, providing the data and insights needed to optimise system performance and ensure it can withstand unexpected disruptions. Embracing load testing and chaos engineering, guided by observability, empowers organisations to deliver more reliable and adaptable software systems in an ever-evolving digital landscape.

9.6 Performance Optimisation Strategies

Optimising system performance is an ongoing effort. We provide a toolkit of performance optimisation strategies, from code-level improvements to architectural changes, all informed by observability insights. These strategies enable teams to continuously enhance the efficiency and responsiveness of their systems.

Performance Optimisation Strategies: A Toolkit for Continuous Improvement

In the fast-paced world of software development, optimising system performance is not a one-time task but an ongoing journey. It requires a holistic approach, encompassing code-level improvements, architectural changes, and a keen reliance on observability insights. This section unveils a toolkit of performance optimisation strategies that enable teams to continually enhance the efficiency and responsiveness of their systems. With observability as our guiding star, we explore various tactics to ensure your applications remain agile and deliver exceptional user experiences.

1. Code-Level Optimisation:

a. Profiling and Benchmarking: Utilise profiling tools to identify performance bottlenecks at the code level. Benchmarking allows you to measure the impact of code changes on performance metrics.

b. Algorithmic Efficiency: Assess and improve the efficiency of algorithms and data structures. Choosing the right data structures and algorithms can significantly impact performance.

c. Memory Management: Optimise memory usage by reducing unnecessary object creation, optimising data structures, and implementing proper resource management.

2. Database Performance:

a. Query Optimisation: Analyse and optimise database queries. Ensure that indexes are appropriately used, and avoid costly join operations or full table scans.

b. Caching: Implement caching mechanisms to reduce the load on the database. Use tools like Redis or Memcached to store frequently accessed data in memory.

c. Connection Pooling: Implement connection pooling to efficiently manage database connections and minimise overhead.

3. Parallelism and Concurrency:

a. Multithreading: Leverage multithreading or multiprocessing to parallelise tasks and utilise available CPU cores effectively.

b. Asynchronous Programming: Use asynchronous programming to handle I/O-bound operations efficiently. It allows applications to perform other tasks while waiting for I/O operations to complete.

c. Concurrency Control: Implement proper concurrency control mechanisms, such as locks or semaphores, to prevent race conditions and ensure thread safety.

4. Infrastructure Scaling:

a. Horizontal Scaling: Add more instances of components to distribute the workload efficiently. Utilise auto-scaling mechanisms in cloud environments.

b. Load Balancing: Implement load balancers to evenly distribute incoming traffic across multiple servers or instances.

5. Caching Strategies:

a. Content Caching: Cache static content, such as images, stylesheets, and JavaScript files, to reduce server load and improve page load times.

b. Query Result Caching: Cache the results of frequently executed database queries to reduce the load on the database.

6. Content Delivery Optimisation:

a. Content Delivery Networks (CDNs): Utilise CDNs to deliver content from geographically distributed edge servers, reducing latency and improving content delivery speed.

b. Minification and Compression: Minimise the size of web assets (e.g., JavaScript and CSS files) and use compression techniques to reduce bandwidth usage.

7. Monitoring and Profiling Tools:

a. Real-time Monitoring: Continuously monitor system performance using observability tools to identify performance issues as they arise.

b. Tracing and Profiling: Use tracing and profiling tools to gain insights into application behaviour, bottlenecks, and resource utilisation.

8. Architectural Changes:

a. Microservices Architecture: Consider transitioning to a microservices architecture to improve scalability and isolate performance bottlenecks.

b. Serverless Computing: Explore serverless computing for event-driven workloads to automatically scale based on demand.

9. Code Review and Refactoring:

a. Code Reviews: Conduct code reviews to identify and address performance-related issues through collaborative feedback.

b. Refactoring: Refactor code to improve readability and maintainability, which can indirectly enhance performance.

10. Resource Management:

a. Resource Cleanup: Ensure proper resource cleanup, such as closing database connections, releasing memory, and closing file handles.

b. Resource Pools: Implement resource pools to efficiently manage and reuse resources, such as database connections or network sockets.

These performance optimisation strategies form a comprehensive toolkit to address a wide range of performance challenges. However, the choice of which strategies to prioritise depends on the specific needs and constraints of your application.

Observability insights are invaluable throughout the performance optimisation process. Real-time monitoring, tracing, and profiling tools provide the data necessary to identify performance bottlenecks and validate the impact of optimisation efforts. By leveraging observability, teams can make data-driven decisions, continuously fine-tune their systems, and ensure that their applications remain agile and responsive In software development.

You will now have a comprehensive understanding of how observability contributes to scalability and performance optimisation. With a better knowledge of how to proactively address performance bottlenecks, plan for capacity, and ensure that systems scale gracefully to meet evolving demands. Observability becomes a strategic asset in maintaining a competitive edge by delivering high-performance, resilient, and responsive software systems.

Chapter 10

Security and Compliance

C hapter 10, is dedicated to exploring the critical intersection of observability, security, and compliance. It sheds light on how observability practices can be leveraged to enhance security measures and ensure that systems adhere to regulatory requirements.

10.1 The Imperative of Security and Compliance

Let's start by underlining the significance of security and compliance in today's interconnected digital landscape. It emphasises how data breaches, vulnerabilities, and non-compliance can result in severe consequences, including financial losses and reputational damage.

The Imperative of Security and Compliance

Security and compliance cannot be overstated. This section serves as a stark reminder of the critical role that security and compliance play in safeguarding organisations and individuals alike. It underscores the potential consequences of neglecting these crucial aspects of the modern digital landscape, including data breaches, vulnerabilities, and non-compliance.

Data Security

Data breaches have become an all too common occurrence in recent years. These breaches involve unauthorised access to sensitive information, often leading to its theft or exposure. The consequences of a data breach can be devastating, both financially and in terms of reputation. Customer trust can erode rapidly when personal information is compromised, and the costs associated with addressing a breach, including legal fees and regulatory fines, can be staggering.

Consider the high-profile data breaches that have made headlines in recent years. From major corporations to government agencies and healthcare providers, no entity is immune to the threat of data breaches. The Equifax breach in 2017, which exposed the personal data of nearly 147 million people, serves as a stark reminder of the far-reaching impact of such incidents. The fallout from this breach included lawsuits, regulatory investigations, and a significant drop in Equifax's stock price.

Vulnerabilities

The digital landscape is constantly evolving, and with it, new vulnerabilities emerge. Cybercriminals are quick to exploit these weaknesses for their gain. Without robust security measures in place, organisations are left exposed to a barrage of threats, ranging from malware and phishing attacks to zero-day vulnerabilities.

Even seemingly innocuous vulnerabilities can have dire consequences. For example, the WannaCry ransomware attack in 2017 exploited a vulnerability in Microsoft's Windows operating system, affecting hundreds of thousands of computers worldwide. The impact was felt across various sectors, from healthcare systems to manufacturing facilities, highlighting the widespread risk associated with unaddressed vulnerabilities.

Non-Compliance

In addition to the threat of breaches and vulnerabilities, organisations must navigate a complex landscape of regulations and compliance requirements. Non-compliance can result in legal actions, fines, and severe damage to an organisation's reputation. Regulations like the General Data Protection Regulation (GDPR) in Europe and the Health Insurance Portability and Accountability Act (HIPAA) in the United States have strict data protection requirements that organisations must adhere to, regardless of their size or industry.

Failure to comply with these regulations can lead to substantial penalties. For instance, GDPR violations can result in fines of up to €20 million or 4% of global annual revenue, whichever is higher. Such penalties can cripple even the largest of enterprises, making compliance a non-negotiable aspect of doing business in today's digital age.

In conclusion, the imperative of security and compliance is paramount in our interconnected digital landscape. Data breaches, vulnerabilities, and non-compliance can have far-reaching and devastating consequences, including financial losses and reputational damage. Organisations must prioritise security and compliance as fundamental elements of their operations to protect themselves, their customers, and their stakeholders from the ever-present threats in the digital realm.

10.2 Observability as a Security Enabler

Observability, when applied strategically, can bolster security efforts in several ways. This section introduces you to the concept of security observability, which involves monitoring and analysing observability data to detect and respond to security threats and vulnerabilities.

Observability as a Security Enabler

Organisations face an ever-expanding array of security threats and vulnerabilities. To effectively protect their systems and data, they must adopt proactive security measures that go beyond traditional methods. This section introduces you to the concept of security observability—a powerful approach that involves monitoring and analysing observability data to detect and respond to security threats and vulnerabilities.

What is Security Observability?

Security observability is an extension of the broader concept of observability, which refers to an organisation's ability to understand, monitor, and troubleshoot the behaviour of its systems and applications. In the context of security, observability focuses on gaining insights into the security posture of an organisation's digital infrastructure.

Security observability involves

Collecting Data: Gathering data from various sources within an organisation's IT environment. This data may include logs, metrics, traces, network traffic, and user behaviour information.

Correlating Data: Analysing and correlating the collected data to identify patterns and anomalies that may indicate security threats or vulnerabilities.

Real-time Monitoring: Continuously monitoring the organisation's systems and applications in real-time to detect security incidents as they occur.

Alerting and Response: Setting up alerts and automated response mechanisms to notify security teams and take immediate action when potential threats are detected.

Benefits of Security Observability

Security observability offers several key benefits as a security enabler:

Early Threat Detection: By continuously monitoring and analysing observability data, organisations can identify security threats in their early stages. This early detection allows for quicker response and mitigation, reducing the potential impact of an attack.

Visibility into Complex Environments: In today's complex IT environments, it can be challenging to gain a comprehensive view of all potential security risks. Security observability provides visibility into every facet of the digital infrastructure, helping organisations spot vulnerabilities and misconfigurations that may otherwise go unnoticed.

Improved Incident Response: Security observability empowers organisations to respond rapidly to security incidents. Automated alerting and response mechanisms can trigger immediate actions, such as isolating affected systems or initiating threat containment measures.

Compliance and Governance: Many regulatory frameworks require organisations to maintain a strong security posture and demonstrate compliance. Security observability aids in meeting these requirements by providing audit trails and evidence of security practices.

Implementing Security Observability

To leverage security observability effectively, organisations should consider the following steps:

Data Collection: Identify the types of data sources relevant to your security needs. These may include logs, application telemetry, network traffic data, and user activity logs.

Data Analysis: Implement tools and processes for analysing the collected data. This may involve the use of machine learning and artificial intelligence (AI) to detect anomalies and patterns associated with security threats.

Alerting and Response: Establish clear alerting criteria and response procedures. Ensure that security teams are well-prepared to respond swiftly to security incidents.

Continuous Improvement: Security observability is an ongoing process. Regularly review and update your observability strategy to adapt to evolving threats and technologies.

Security observability is a valuable approach that empowers organisations to proactively detect and respond to security threats and vulnerabilities. By leveraging observability data, organisations can enhance their security posture, reduce the impact of security incidents, and better protect their digital assets and sensitive data in an increasingly hostile digital landscape.

10.3 Monitoring Security Events

Effective security observability requires monitoring for security events and anomalies in metrics, traces, and logs. You will gain insights into how to set up alerts and anomaly detection mechanisms to identify unauthorised access, data breaches, and other security incidents.

Monitoring Security Events

To achieve effective security observability, organisations must implement robust monitoring systems that continuously track security events and anomalies across various data sources, including metrics, traces, and logs. In this section, you will gain insights into how to set up alerts and anomaly detection mechanisms to identify unauthorised access, data breaches, and other security incidents.

Setting Up Alerts

Setting up alerts is a fundamental aspect of security event monitoring. Alerts serve as real-time notifications that inform security teams of potentially suspicious or malicious activities. Here's how organisations can set up alerts effectively:

Identify Critical Events: Determine which security events are critical to monitor. These may include failed login attempts, unusual data access patterns, changes in user privileges, and suspicious network traffic.

Thresholds and Triggers: Define thresholds and triggers for alert generation. For instance, if a certain number of failed login attempts occur within a specific time frame, an alert should be triggered.

Alert Severity Levels: Assign severity levels to alerts to prioritise incident response efforts. High-severity alerts may require immediate attention, while lower-severity alerts can be investigated as time allows.

Automated Alerts: Implement automated alerting systems that send notifications to designated personnel or teams. Automation ensures that alerts are acted upon promptly.

Anomaly Detection

Anomaly detection is a critical component of security event

monitoring, as it helps identify deviations from normal behaviour. Here's how organisations can implement anomaly detection mechanisms:

Baseline Establishment: Establish a baseline of normal system and user behaviour. This baseline is derived from historical data and defines what is considered typical.

Machine Learning and AI: Utilise machine learning and artificial intelligence techniques to detect anomalies. These algorithms can identify patterns and anomalies in large datasets, making it possible to detect unusual activities that may signify security threats.

Behavioural Analysis: Conduct behavioural analysis of users and systems. Look for deviations from established patterns, such as users accessing resources they don't typically use or systems exhibiting unusual resource consumption.

Contextual Anomaly Detection: Consider contextual information when evaluating anomalies. For example, an employee accessing sensitive data during non-working hours might raise a red flag, even if the access itself appears legitimate.

Integration of Logs, Metrics, and Traces

To achieve comprehensive security observability, organisations should integrate data from various sources, including logs, metrics, and traces:

Logs: Logs contain detailed records of system and application activities. Centralise log data from different sources, such as operating systems, applications, and network devices, to gain a holistic view of security events.

Metrics: Metrics provide quantitative data about system performance and behaviour. Monitor metrics such as CPU usage, memory utilisation, and network traffic to detect anomalies that may indicate security incidents.

Traces: Distributed tracing can help identify security-related issues in microservices or complex applications. Trace requests across services to identify bottlenecks, errors, or unauthorised access.

Response and Mitigation

Effective security event monitoring doesn't stop at detection; it also involves response and mitigation:

Incident Response Plans: Develop incident response plans that outline the steps to be taken when a security event is detected. Assign responsibilities and establish communication channels for incident response.

Automated Response: Consider automating response actions for specific types of security events. For example, in the case of a detected brute-force attack, an automated response could include blocking the source IP address.

Continuous Improvement: Regularly review and improve the monitoring and alerting systems based on lessons learned from security incidents. Adapt to evolving threats and technologies.

In conclusion, monitoring security events is a critical component of security observability. By setting up alerts and implementing anomaly detection mechanisms, organisations can proactively identify and respond to unauthorised access, data breaches, and other security incidents, ultimately enhancing their overall security posture.

10.4 Detecting Vulnerabilities

Vulnerability detection is a critical aspect of security observability. The section discusses strategies for monitoring and analysing observability data to identify vulnerabilities in software, applications, and infrastructure components. It also explores how observability can contribute to proactive vulnerability management.

Detecting Vulnerabilities

Detecting vulnerabilities is a crucial part of maintaining a strong security posture, and it's an integral aspect of security observability. This section explores strategies for monitoring and analysing observability data to identify vulnerabilities in software, applications, and infrastructure components. It also highlights how observability can contribute to proactive vulnerability management.

Monitoring Software and Infrastructure Components

To effectively detect vulnerabilities, organisations should implement continuous monitoring of their software and infrastructure. This involves the following strategies:

Patch Management: Keep software, operating systems, and third-party applications up-to-date with the latest security patches. Automated patch management tools can help ensure timely updates.

Vulnerability Scanning: Regularly scan systems and applications for known vulnerabilities using vulnerability scanning tools. These tools can identify missing patches, misconfigurations, and other weaknesses.

Configuration Auditing: Perform regular audits of system configurations to identify deviations from security best practices. This helps identify misconfigurations that could be exploited.

Observability Data for Vulnerability Detection

Observability data can be a valuable resource for identifying vulnerabilities. Here's how to leverage observability for this purpose:

Logs: Analyse logs for error messages, unusual access patterns, or signs of attempted exploitation. For example, repeated login failures may indicate a brute-force attack.

Metrics: Monitor system metrics for anomalies that might signify a vulnerability. Unusual CPU or memory usage could indicate a software flaw or a malware infection.

Traces: In distributed systems, trace requests to identify potential vulnerabilities in microservices or API endpoints. Look for patterns of unexpected behaviour or unauthorised access.

Anomaly Detection for Vulnerabilities

Implementing anomaly detection techniques can help identify vulnerabilities based on deviations from normal behaviour:

Behavioural Analysis: Analyse the behaviour of software and systems to identify deviations from established patterns. For instance, if a web application suddenly starts making an unusual number of database queries, it might indicate a SQL injection vulnerability.

User Behaviour Analysis: Monitor user activity to detect unauthorised access or suspicious behaviour. Identify unusual login times, multiple login failures, or attempts to access restricted areas.

Network Traffic Analysis: Analyse network traffic for unusual patterns, such as an increase in traffic to a particular port or a sudden spike in outbound data. These could indicate a network-based vulnerability or a breach.

Proactive Vulnerability Management

To proactively manage vulnerabilities, organisations should adopt a structured approach:

Vulnerability Assessment: Regularly assess the organisation's infrastructure and applications for vulnerabilities. Prioritise vulnerabilities based on severity and potential impact.

Remediation: Develop a remediation plan that includes patching, configuration changes, or other mitigations for identified vulnerabilities. Implement a risk-based approach, addressing the most critical vulnerabilities first.

Monitoring Progress: Continuously monitor the progress of vulnerability remediation efforts. Ensure that vulnerabilities are closed within a reasonable timeframe.

Vulnerability Intelligence: Stay informed about emerging vulnerabilities by subscribing to vulnerability databases and security advisories. This information is critical for proactive vulnerability management.

In conclusion, detecting vulnerabilities is a critical component of security observability. By continuously monitoring observability data, analysing logs, metrics, and traces, and applying anomaly detection techniques, organisations can identify vulnerabilities in their software, applications, and infrastructure components. Proactive vulnerability management, including timely remediation, helps organisations reduce their attack surface and enhance their overall security posture.

10.5 Compliance Monitoring and Reporting

For organisations subject to regulatory requirements, compliance monitoring is a crucial aspect of observability. The section outlines how observability data can be leveraged to demonstrate compliance with data protection regulations, industry standards, and best practices. This ensures that organisations can provide the necessary audit trails and reports to meet compliance obligations.

Compliance Monitoring and Reporting

For organisations subject to regulatory requirements, compliance monitoring is a crucial aspect of security observability. This section outlines how observability data can be leveraged to demonstrate compliance with data protection regulations, industry standards, and best practices. This ensures that organisations can provide the necessary audit trails and reports to meet their compliance obligations.

Regulatory Compliance and Observability

Compliance with data protection regulations such as GDPR, HIPAA, or industry-specific standards like PCI DSS is mandatory for many organisations. Observability plays a vital role in meeting these compliance requirements by providing the necessary visibility and auditability:

Data Handling: Observability can track how sensitive data is handled within an organisation, including who accesses it, when, and for what purpose.

Security Controls: Monitoring security controls, such as access controls, encryption, and authentication mechanisms, helps ensure that these controls are functioning as required by regulations.

Incident Response: Observability data aids in demonstrating that an organisation has a well-defined incident response plan and can provide evidence of incident investigations, mitigations, and reporting.

Leveraging Observability Data for Compliance

To leverage observability data effectively for compliance monitoring and reporting, organisations can consider the following strategies:

Data Collection and Retention: Collect and retain observability data in accordance with regulatory requirements. Ensure that data is kept for the required retention periods.

Access Controls: Use observability data to track and audit access to sensitive information. Implement strict access controls to limit access to authorised personnel only.

Change Monitoring: Track changes to configurations, permissions, and user privileges. Changes should be logged, reviewed, and authorised in compliance with industry standards.

Incident Logging: Maintain comprehensive logs of security incidents and breaches. These logs should include details about the incident, the response, and any actions taken to prevent future occurrences.

Compliance Reporting

Compliance reporting involves the generation of reports and documentation to demonstrate adherence to regulatory requirements and standards. Observability data can be instrumental in producing these reports:

Auditing Trails: Observability data provides audit trails that can be used to reconstruct events, access history, and changes to configurations. These trails are crucial for demonstrating compliance during audits.

Automated Reporting: Implement automated reporting mechanisms that generate compliance reports on a regular basis. These reports can be customised to match the specific requirements of the regulations or standards in question.

Evidence Collection: Use observability data as evidence during audits or assessments. Ensure that data is readily accessible and organised to facilitate the audit process.

Continuous Monitoring: Compliance is an ongoing process. Implement continuous monitoring of observability data to ensure that compliance is maintained over time and to quickly identify and address any deviations.

Third-Party Compliance Tools

Consider using third-party compliance tools that integrate with your observability systems. These tools can automate the process of collecting, analysing, and reporting on observability data in a way that aligns with regulatory requirements.

Training and Documentation

Ensure that personnel responsible for observability data collection and reporting are adequately trained in compliance requirements. Maintain clear documentation of your observability practices and procedures to demonstrate your commitment to compliance.

In conclusion, compliance monitoring and reporting are essential aspects of security observability, especially for organisations subject to regulatory requirements. By leveraging observability data effectively, organisations can demonstrate their adherence to data protection regulations, industry standards, and best practices, thereby ensuring they meet their compliance obligations and avoid legal and financial repercussions.

10.6 Incident Response and Forensics

When security incidents occur, observability data is invaluable for incident response and forensics. you will learn how to use observability insights to investigate security breaches, identify the root causes, and implement corrective measures to prevent recurrence.

Incident Response and Forensics with Observability Data

When security incidents occur, observability data becomes invaluable for incident response and forensics. In this section, you will learn how to leverage observability insights to investigate security breaches, identify root causes, and implement corrective measures to prevent recurrence.

Incident Response with Observability Data

Effective incident response relies on rapid detection, containment, investigation, and recovery. Observability data plays a crucial role in each of these phases:

Detection: Observability data, including logs, metrics, and traces, can trigger alerts and notifications when unusual or malicious activities are detected. Early detection is vital for minimising the impact of an incident.

Containment: After detecting an incident, organisations can use observability data to isolate affected systems or networks to prevent further compromise. This containment is crucial to stop the incident from spreading.

Investigation: Observability data provides a wealth of information to investigate incidents. Security teams can analyse logs to understand the timeline of events, trace user activity, and identify the attack vectors used by adversaries.

Recovery: After containing and investigating the incident, observability data can help assess the extent of damage and guide recovery efforts. Metrics can show the impact on system performance, while logs can reveal data exfiltration or unauthorised access.

Forensics Analysis

Forensics analysis is the process of collecting, preserving, and analysing digital evidence to understand how a security incident occurred and who may have been responsible. Observability data is a crucial source of forensic evidence:

Log Analysis: Logs are a primary source of evidence in forensic investigations. Security teams can reconstruct events by analysing logs from affected systems, applications, and network devices.

Chain of Custody: Observability data can establish a chain of custody for digital evidence, ensuring that the integrity and authenticity of evidence are maintained, which is critical for legal purposes.

Timeline Reconstruction: Observability data can help create a timeline of events, allowing investigators to piece together the sequence of actions taken by the attacker and the response efforts.

Root Cause Analysis: Forensics analysis with observability data seeks to identify the root causes of an incident. It can reveal vulnerabilities, misconfigurations, or lapses in security controls that allowed the incident to occur.

Corrective Measures and Prevention

After conducting an incident response and forensics analysis, organisations must take corrective measures to prevent recurrence and strengthen their security posture:

Patch and Remediate: Address vulnerabilities and misconfigurations identified during the investigation. Implement patches, updates, and configuration changes to eliminate weaknesses.

Improved Security Controls: Enhance security controls based on lessons learned. This may include improving access controls, implementing multi-factor authentication, or revising security policies.

User Awareness and Training: Educate employees and users

about security best practices and the importance of following security protocols to prevent future incidents.

Continual Improvement: Use the insights gained from the incident response and forensics process to continually improve security practices and incident response plans.

Documentation and Reporting

Maintain comprehensive documentation of the incident response and forensics process, including findings, actions taken, and lessons learned. This documentation is vital for regulatory compliance, legal proceedings, and improving incident response practices.

Automation and Orchestration

Consider automating incident response processes and incorporating observability data into security orchestration workflows. Automation can help organisations respond more rapidly to incidents and reduce the impact.

In conclusion, observability data is an invaluable asset for incident response and forensics analysis. Organisations must be prepared to leverage this data to detect and respond to security incidents effectively, conduct thorough forensics investigations, and implement corrective measures to prevent future breaches and strengthen their overall security posture.

10.7 Security and Compliance Best Practices

The section concludes with a collection of best practices for integrating observability into security and compliance strategies. These practices encompass the proactive monitoring of security events, continuous vulnerability assessment, and adherence to compliance frameworks.

Security and Compliance Best Practices with Observability

In conclusion, integrating observability into security and compliance strategies is crucial for organisations aiming to maintain a strong security posture and meet regulatory requirements. The following best practices encompass proactive monitoring of security events, continuous vulnerability assessment, and adherence to compliance frameworks:

1. Comprehensive Data Collection

- Collect observability data from various sources, including logs, metrics, traces, and network traffic. Ensure that data is centralised, easily accessible, and well-organised.

2. Real-time Monitoring and Alerts

- Implement real-time monitoring of observability data to detect security events and anomalies as they occur. Set up alerts and notifications to notify security teams promptly.

3. Continuous Vulnerability Assessment

- Regularly scan systems and applications for vulnerabilities using automated tools. Prioritise vulnerabilities based on severity and potential impact.

4. Anomaly Detection

- Leverage anomaly detection techniques to identify deviations from normal behaviour. This can help detect security threats and vulnerabilities early.

5. Integration of Observability Data

- Integrate observability data from various sources to gain a holistic view of your digital infrastructure. Logs, metrics, and traces should complement each other in security and compliance efforts.

6. Compliance Monitoring and Reporting

- Establish processes for compliance monitoring and reporting. Automate compliance reporting where possible to ensure accurate and timely submissions.

7. Incident Response Plan

- Develop a well-defined incident response plan that includes procedures for detecting, containing, investigating, and recovering from security incidents. Ensure that observability data plays a central role in this plan.

8. Forensics Analysis

- Conduct thorough forensics analysis using observability data to understand the root causes of security incidents. This analysis helps prevent future breaches.

9. Patch Management

- Maintain a robust patch management process to keep software, operating systems, and third-party applications up-to-date with security patches.

10. Access Controls

- Implement strict access controls to limit access to sensitive data and resources. Monitor user privileges and access patterns.

11. Configuration Management

- Regularly audit system configurations to identify and remediate misconfigurations that may expose vulnerabilities.

12. User Training and Awareness

- Train employees and users on security best practices and the importance of following security protocols. Encourage a culture of security awareness.

13. Compliance Frameworks

- Familiarise yourself with relevant compliance frameworks and regulations, such as GDPR, HIPAA, or PCI DSS. Ensure that your observability practices align with these requirements.

14. Automation and Orchestration

- Automate incident response processes and integrate observability data into security orchestration workflows to streamline response efforts.

15. Continuous Improvement

- Continually review and improve observability practices based on lessons learned from security incidents and compliance audits. Adapt to evolving threats and technologies.

By incorporating these best practices into their security and compliance strategies, organisations can effectively leverage observability data to enhance their security posture, maintain compliance, and mitigate risks in an ever-evolving digital landscape.

Hopefully you will now have a comprehensive understanding of how observability can be harnessed to enhance security and compliance efforts. You are equipped with the knowledge and tools to proactively monitor for security threats, detect vulnerabilities, and ensure that systems remain in compliance with regulatory requirements. Observability becomes a strategic asset in safeguarding data, protecting against threats, and maintaining trust with customers and stakeholders.

Chapter 11

Building a Culture of Observability

C hapter 11, explores the critical aspects of building a culture of observability within organisations. It delves into the mindset, practices, and collaboration needed to foster an observability-centric approach that permeates every facet of an organisation.

Team Culture

11.1 The Culture of Observability

The chapter begins by defining what it means to have a culture of observability. It underscores how this culture is not limited to technical teams but extends to all levels of an organisation, from leadership to development, operations, and support.

The Culture of Observability

Observability has become a buzzword in the world of technology and operations, but it's more than just a trendy term. It represents a fundamental shift in how organisations approach monitoring, troubleshooting, and understanding their systems. Observability is not just a set of tools or practices; it's a culture that permeates all levels of an organisation. In this section, we will explore what it means to have a culture of observability and why it is essential for modern businesses.

To start, let's define what we mean by a culture of observability. At its core, this culture is centred around the idea that gaining insights into your systems' behaviour should be a shared responsibility, not limited to a select few technical experts. It's about fostering an environment where everyone, from leadership to development, operations, and support teams, actively participates in the process of understanding and improving the systems that drive the business.

In a culture of observability, there are several key principles that guide the organisation:

1. Transparency: The first pillar of observability culture is transparency. This means that data, metrics, logs, and other relevant information about systems and processes are readily available to anyone who needs them. There are no hidden silos of information, and data is not hoarded by specific teams or individuals. This transparency empowers everyone to make informed decisions based on real-time information.

2. Collaboration: Observability is a team sport. It encourages collaboration across different departments and teams. When an issue arises, it's not just the operations team's problem or the developers' responsibility to fix it. Instead, everyone works together to diagnose the problem, understand its impact, and find a solution. This collaborative approach leads to quicker

resolutions and a deeper understanding of the systems.

3. Learning and Improvement: A culture of observability is built on a continuous learning mindset. When something goes wrong, it's not seen as a failure but as an opportunity to learn and improve. Post-incident reviews, blameless retrospectives, and knowledge sharing sessions become common practices. These activities help the organisation become more resilient and adaptive in the face of challenges.

4. Automation: Automation plays a significant role in observability culture. It's not about replacing humans with machines but using automation to handle routine tasks, gather data, and provide alerts. This frees up human resources to focus on more complex problem-solving and creative tasks.

5. Customer-Centric: Ultimately, the goal of observability is to improve the customer experience. A culture of observability keeps the customer at the centre of every decision and action. By monitoring and understanding how systems impact customers, organisations can make data-driven decisions to enhance their products and services continually.

6. Leadership Support: Leadership sets the tone for the entire organisation. In a culture of observability, leaders actively promote and support these principles. They invest in the necessary tools and resources, encourage experimentation, and prioritise learning and improvement over blame.

Having a culture of observability is not a one-time effort; it's an ongoing journey. Organisations must invest in training, tools, and processes to nurture this culture. The benefits are significant—faster problem resolution, reduced downtime, improved customer satisfaction, and a more resilient business overall.

In conclusion, a culture of observability is not limited to technical teams; it's a mindset that should permeate every aspect of an organisation. It's about transparency, collaboration, learning, and automation, all focused on delivering the best possible experience to customers. Embracing this culture is crucial for organisations looking to thrive in today's complex and fast-paced business environment.

11.2 Leadership and Buy-In

Effective observability starts at the top. The section discusses the importance of leadership buy-in and how executives and managers play a pivotal role in championing observability initiatives. It also highlights strategies for making a compelling business case for observability investments.

Leadership and Buy-In: Championing Observability Initiatives

In the journey towards establishing a culture of observability, one of the most critical factors is securing buy-in from leadership and top-level executives. This section explores the indispensable role that leadership plays in championing observability initiatives and outlines strategies for making a compelling business case for observability investments.

1. Setting the Vision:
   Effective observability initiatives start with a clear and compelling vision set by leadership. Executives must understand and articulate the value of observability in achieving business objectives. They should define the strategic goals and expectations tied to observability and communicate these to the entire organisation.

2. Resource Allocation:
   Leaders play a pivotal role in allocating resources, both financial and human, for observability efforts. This includes budgeting for tools, training, and personnel. Leadership's commitment to providing these resources sends a strong signal that observability is a priority.

3. Culture Transformation:

Culture change often begins at the top. Executives and managers should lead by example, embracing observability practices and encouraging their teams to do the same. Their active participation in observability initiatives can influence others throughout the organisation.

4. Communication and Advocacy:

Effective leadership is about advocacy and communication. Leaders should be vocal advocates for observability, consistently communicating its importance and benefits to all stakeholders. They should also highlight successes and share stories that demonstrate how observability positively impacts the business.

5. Making the Business Case:

To secure buy-in from leadership, it's essential to make a compelling business case for observability investments. This case should focus on the tangible benefits, such as reduced downtime, improved customer satisfaction, and faster incident resolution. Data and metrics should support these claims.

a. Quantifying Impact: Use data to quantify the impact of observability on key performance indicators (KPIs). Show how observability can lead to cost savings, revenue increases, or risk mitigation.

b. Demonstrating ROI: Calculate the return on investment (ROI) for observability initiatives. Compare the expected benefits to the costs involved. Presenting a clear ROI can be persuasive to decision-makers.

c. Highlighting Competitive Advantage: Emphasise how observability can provide a competitive advantage. In today's fast-paced digital landscape, organisations that can quickly detect and address issues gain an edge.

d. Mitigating Risks: Discuss how observability can help mitigate risks, such as security breaches or compliance violations. Highlighting the potential consequences of not investing in observability can be a strong motivator.

6. Pilots and Proof of Concept: Leadership may be more inclined to support observability initiatives if they see evidence of success. Consider starting with small-scale pilots or proof-of-concept projects to demonstrate the value of observability before scaling up.

7. Continuous Engagement: Securing leadership buy-in is not a one-time effort. It requires continuous engagement. Regularly update executives on the progress of observability initiatives and the impact on business outcomes.

In conclusion, leadership buy-in is a critical driver of successful observability initiatives. Executives and managers set the tone for the organisation's observability culture, allocate resources, and make critical decisions. To secure their support, it's crucial to articulate a compelling business case that demonstrates how observability aligns with strategic objectives and delivers measurable value. With leadership backing, the journey towards a culture of observability becomes smoother and more effective.

11.3 Collaboration and Cross-Functional Teams

Observability thrives in environments where collaboration is encouraged. You will learn about the benefits of cross-functional teams, where individuals from different disciplines work together to ensure observability is embedded into the fabric of the organisation.

Collaboration and Cross-Functional Teams: Building Observability into the Organisation's Fabric

Observability isn't just a technical concern; it's a mindset that requires collaboration across diverse teams and disciplines. In this section, we will explore the profound benefits of cross-functional teams and how they play a pivotal role in ensuring that observability becomes an integral part of an organisation's culture.

Diverse Expertise: Cross-functional teams bring together individuals from different backgrounds and areas of expertise. This diversity of skills and perspectives enriches problem-solving and fosters innovation. When tackling observability challenges, these teams can offer a well-rounded approach that considers various aspects of the system.

Holistic Understanding: Observability is about gaining a holistic understanding of complex systems. Cross-functional teams are better equipped to achieve this because they can explore and analyse systems from multiple angles. Developers, operations experts, data analysts, and customer support professionals can all contribute unique insights to the observability effort.

Faster Problem Resolution: Complex issues often require collaboration across departments. Cross-functional teams can quickly diagnose and resolve problems by leveraging the collective knowledge and skills of their members. This leads to shorter downtime and improved system reliability.

Shared Responsibility: Observability is most effective when it's a shared responsibility. Cross-functional teams promote this ethos by ensuring that everyone is actively engaged in monitoring, analysing, and improving system performance. This shared ownership reduces the burden on any one team and fosters a sense of accountability.

Knowledge Transfer: Cross-functional teams facilitate knowledge transfer between different parts of the organisation. For example, when developers work closely with operations teams, they gain insights into the operational challenges of their code, leading to more robust and maintainable applications. This knowledge sharing enhances overall system observability.

Continuous Improvement: Observability is not a one-time effort but an ongoing process of improvement. Cross-functional teams are well-positioned to lead post-incident reviews, retrospectives, and knowledge-sharing sessions. These activities drive continuous improvement and help the organisation learn from its experiences.

Efficient Communication: Effective communication is critical in observability efforts. Cross-functional teams encourage open and transparent communication, breaking down silos that can hinder the flow of information. When everyone is on the same page, it becomes easier to detect and respond to issues.

Innovation and Creativity: Cross-functional teams foster an environment where innovation and creativity can thrive. When individuals from different disciplines collaborate, they bring fresh perspectives and ideas to the table. This can lead to innovative solutions for observability challenges.

Customer-Centric Approach: Observability should always be aligned with improving the customer experience. Cross-functional teams ensure that the customer perspective is integrated into every aspect of observability, from monitoring application performance to resolving incidents promptly.

Scalability and Adaptability: As organisations grow and evolve, cross-functional teams are adaptable and scalable. They can adjust their composition and focus to meet changing business needs and technology landscapes.

In conclusion, cross-functional teams are the backbone of building observability into an organisation's fabric. They leverage diverse expertise, promote shared responsibility, and drive continuous improvement. By fostering collaboration across different disciplines, organisations can create a culture of observability that not only enhances system reliability but also drives innovation and delivers exceptional experiences to customers.

11.4 Training and Skill Development

To foster a culture of observability, organisations need to invest in training and skill development. This section provides guidance on creating training programs that empower team members to become proficient in observability tools and practices.

Training and Skill Development: Empowering a Culture of Observability

In the quest to foster a culture of observability, one of the crucial pillars is investing in training and skill development. This section sheds light on the significance of creating training programs that empower team members to become proficient in observability tools and practices.

Understanding the Importance of Training:
The first step in building a culture of observability through training is recognising its importance. Training equips team members with the knowledge and skills necessary to effectively use observability tools and practices. It empowers them to contribute to the organisation's overall observability goals.

Tailored Training Programs:
Not all teams or individuals require the same level of training. Tailor your training programs to meet the specific needs of different roles within your organisation. For example, developers may need training on instrumenting code for observability, while operations teams may require training on monitoring and alerting.

Hands-On Learning:
Effective observability training should include hands-on learning experiences. Instead of solely relying on theoretical

concepts, provide opportunities for participants to work with real observability tools and data. Practical experience is often the best teacher.

Certifications and Credentials:

Consider offering certifications or credentials related to observability. These can serve as a valuable benchmark of proficiency and can be a motivating factor for team members to complete training programs. Industry-recognised certifications can also enhance an individual's career prospects.

Continuous Learning Culture: Observability is not static; it evolves as technology and systems change. Encourage a culture of continuous learning by providing ongoing training opportunities. Host regular workshops, webinars, and knowledge-sharing sessions to keep team members up to date.

Mentoring and Peer Learning:

Peer learning and mentoring programs can be highly effective. Experienced team members can mentor newcomers, sharing their knowledge and expertise. This not only accelerates learning but also promotes a sense of community and collaboration.

Integration with Workflow:

Make observability training an integral part of your team's workflow. When team members see how observability tools and practices directly impact their day-to-day tasks, they are more likely to embrace them.

Feedback and Assessment:

Gather feedback from participants to continuously improve training programs. Regular assessments can help identify areas where individuals may need additional support. Use this feedback loop to refine your training approach.

Resource Library:

Create a resource library that team members can access

for reference. This library can include documentation, best practices, and training materials, making it easier for team members to refresh their knowledge when needed.

Cross-Functional Training:

Encourage cross-functional training to foster collaboration and a shared understanding of observability. For example, developers can attend training sessions led by operations experts, and vice versa, to gain a deeper appreciation of each other's challenges and perspectives.

Incentives and Recognition:

Recognise and reward team members who excel in observability training. Incentives such as bonuses, promotions, or public recognition can motivate individuals to invest in their observability skills.

Measurement and ROI:

Measure the impact of your training programs by tracking observability-related metrics such as incident resolution time, system availability, and customer satisfaction. Demonstrating a positive return on investment (ROI) from training can help secure ongoing support and resources.

In conclusion, training and skill development are vital components of nurturing a culture of observability. By investing in well-designed training programs, organisations empower their team members to effectively leverage observability tools and practices, driving better system performance, faster issue resolution, and ultimately, a more resilient and customer-centric organisation.

11.5 Feedback Loops and Continuous Improvement

Feedback loops are essential for ongoing improvement. The

section explores how organisations can establish mechanisms for gathering feedback from observability data and using it to drive continuous improvement in systems and processes.

Feedback Loops and Continuous Improvement: Harnessing Observability Data

In the pursuit of a culture of observability, establishing feedback loops is paramount. This section delves into the importance of feedback mechanisms that enable organisations to gather insights from observability data and apply them to drive continuous improvement in their systems and processes.

The Power of Feedback Loops:
Feedback loops are the lifeblood of any observability-driven organisation. They are the means by which data transforms into actionable insights, allowing teams to adapt and enhance their systems and practices continually.

Data-Driven Decision-Making:
Observability provides a wealth of data about system behaviour, performance, and user experiences. Feedback loops enable organisations to harness this data for informed decision-making. Rather than relying on gut instincts, decisions are based on concrete evidence.

Incident Post-Mortems:
After an incident or outage, feedback loops come into play through post-mortem or post-incident reviews. These reviews are a structured way to analyse what went wrong, why it happened, and how similar issues can be prevented in the future. They are instrumental in driving improvements.

Root Cause Analysis:
Feedback loops help organisations perform root cause analyses. Instead of treating symptoms, they dig deeper to identify the underlying causes of problems. Addressing root causes leads to more effective solutions.

Customer Feedback Integration:

Observability data should not exist in isolation. Feedback loops should include mechanisms for integrating customer feedback. Understanding how system performance affects users is crucial for making customer-centric improvements.

Automated Alerts and Notifications:

Observability tools can provide automated alerts and notifications based on predefined thresholds or anomalies. These alerts serve as real-time feedback, allowing teams to proactively address issues before they impact users.

Feedback from Cross-Functional Teams:

Cross-functional teams play a vital role in feedback loops. Developers, operations, and support teams should provide feedback on observability data. Their diverse perspectives help uncover insights that might otherwise be missed.

Continuous Monitoring and Analysis:

Observability is not a one-time activity. Continuous monitoring and analysis are essential components of feedback loops. Organisations should regularly review data and performance metrics to identify trends, anomalies, and areas for improvement.

Benchmarking and Comparison:

Feedback loops enable organisations to benchmark their current performance against past performance and industry standards. Comparing data over time helps identify areas that need attention.

Experimentation and Iteration:

Feedback loops support a culture of experimentation and iteration. Teams can use observability data to experiment with changes and assess their impact. The iterative process allows for gradual improvements without disrupting operations.

Documentation and Knowledge Sharing:

Documenting insights gained from feedback loops and sharing them across the organisation is crucial. This ensures that knowledge is not lost and that improvements are widely understood and implemented.

Feedback Loop Metrics:
Define and track metrics related to the effectiveness of feedback loops. Are issues being resolved more quickly? Are incident recurrence rates decreasing? Use these metrics to measure the impact of feedback-driven improvements.

Adaptive Systems:
Feedback loops can also drive the development of adaptive systems that can self-adjust in response to changing conditions. This is particularly important in dynamic and fast-paced environments.

In conclusion, feedback loops are the bridge between observability data and continuous improvement. They allow organisations to respond to challenges, optimise their systems and processes, and deliver better experiences to their customers. By nurturing effective feedback mechanisms, organisations can evolve into more resilient, agile, and customer-focused entities.

11.6 Measuring Success

Success in observability initiatives should be measurable. The section explores key performance indicators (KPIs) and metrics that can be used to assess the effectiveness of observability practices and their impact on system reliability, performance, and security.

Measuring Success in Observability Initiatives: Key Performance Indicators (KPIs) and Metrics

Success in observability initiatives is not only attainable but also measurable. This section delves into the critical role of Key Performance Indicators (KPIs) and metrics in assessing the effectiveness of observability practices and their impact on system reliability, performance, and security.

System Availability:
- Metric: Uptime Percentage
- KPI: Achieving a high system uptime percentage indicates that observability practices are effective in quickly detecting and mitigating issues, minimising downtime, and ensuring a stable system.

Incident Response Time:
- Metric: Mean Time to Detect (MTTD) and Mean Time to Resolve (MTTR)
- KPI: Reducing MTTD and MTTR signifies that observability tools and processes enable swift incident detection and resolution, minimising service disruptions.

Customer Satisfaction:
- Metric: Customer Feedback Scores
- KPI: High customer satisfaction scores are indicative of a positive user experience, often linked to reliable systems enabled by observability.

Issue Detection and Alerts:
- Metric: False Positive Rate
- KPI: A low false positive rate indicates that observability tools are effective at alerting only when genuine issues occur, reducing alert fatigue and focusing efforts on real problems.

Security and Compliance:
- Metric: Number of Security Incidents and Compliance Violations
- KPI: Reducing the number of security incidents and compliance violations showcases the role of observability in maintaining a secure and compliant environment.

Capacity Planning:
- Metric: Resource Utilisation and Trend Analysis

- KPI: Accurate capacity planning and resource optimisation demonstrate how observability helps in efficiently managing resources and scaling systems.

Error Rates:
  - Metric: Error Rates and Error Trend Analysis
  - KPI: Reducing error rates and spotting trends in error occurrence highlights the effectiveness of observability in maintaining system quality.

Incident Recurrence:
  - Metric: Incident Recurrence Rate
  - KPI: A decrease in incident recurrence rates shows that observability-driven improvements are effective in preventing the same issues from reoccurring.

Resource Costs:
  - Metric: Cost Savings
  - KPI: Demonstrating cost savings in terms of reduced infrastructure and operational costs, as well as improved resource allocation, indicates the economic benefits of observability.

Change Impact Assessment:
  - Metric: Change-Related Incidents
  - KPI: A reduction in incidents related to changes in the system indicates that observability helps in assessing and mitigating risks associated with updates and deployments.

Monitoring Coverage:
  - Metric: Percentage of Monitored Components
  - KPI: Increasing monitoring coverage ensures that all critical components are observed, contributing to proactive issue identification.

Feedback Loop Efficiency:
  - Metric: Time to Implement Feedback-Driven Improvements
  - KPI: A shorter time between identifying issues through

feedback loops and implementing improvements suggests a responsive and agile observability culture.

Training Impact:
- Metric: Proficiency Scores
- KPI: Improvements in proficiency scores following observability training programs demonstrate the effectiveness of skill development efforts.

Response to Security Incidents:
- Metric: Time to Remediate Security Vulnerabilities
- KPI: Rapid response and remediation of security incidents are crucial indicators of observability's role in maintaining a secure environment.

Capacity for Growth:
- Metric: Scalability
- KPI: Observability practices should support the organisation's growth without compromising performance, security, or reliability.

In conclusion, success in observability initiatives is measurable through a range of KPIs and metrics that assess the impact on system reliability, performance, and security. By regularly monitoring and analysing these indicators, organisations can refine their observability practices, drive continuous improvement, and achieve the desired outcomes of a resilient and customer-centric technology ecosystem.

11.7 Case Studies and Success Stories

To illustrate the concepts discussed, the section presents real-world case studies and success stories from organisations that have successfully built a culture of observability. These examples showcase the tangible benefits of an observability-centric culture in action.

Case Studies and Success Stories: Real-World Examples of Observability Success

In this section, we'll delve into a handful of light real-world case studies and success stories from organisations that have successfully embraced and implemented a culture of observability. For the full versions of these case studies and more resources you can find them on my website **danielsalt.com**

For now these examples highlight the tangible benefits and transformative power of observability practices in action.

1. **Netflix**: Resilience through Chaos Engineering
   - Background: Netflix is renowned for its observability practices. They have implemented Chaos Engineering, where they intentionally inject failures into their systems to test their resilience.
   - Outcome: By actively seeking out weaknesses and addressing them proactively, Netflix has achieved remarkable system reliability. They've minimised downtime and optimised user experiences even during unexpected incidents.

2. **Etsy**: Real-time Monitoring for Rapid Issue Resolution
   - Background: Etsy, the online marketplace, heavily relies on observability to maintain high availability for its millions of users.
   - Outcome: Through real-time monitoring and a strong observability culture, Etsy has reduced its mean time to detect and resolve issues significantly. Their proactive approach has led to a more reliable platform and improved customer satisfaction.

3. **Slack**: Incident Response Efficiency
   - Background: Slack, a widely used collaboration tool, places a strong emphasis on incident response and observability.
   - Outcome: By integrating observability into their incident response workflows, Slack has reduced the time it takes to

diagnose and resolve issues. This has helped them maintain a highly available service for their users.

4.**Twitter**: Scaling with Confidence
- Background: Twitter handles an enormous amount of real-time data. Observability is critical to ensure that the platform scales reliably.
- Outcome: Twitter's observability practices have allowed them to confidently handle massive traffic spikes during major events, such as live broadcasts and trending topics. This has helped them avoid service disruptions and maintain user trust.

5. **Shopify:** Data-Driven Decision-Making
- Background: Shopify, an e-commerce platform, relies on observability to make data-driven decisions and optimise its services.
- Outcome: By leveraging observability data, Shopify has improved system performance, reduced errors, and enhanced the customer shopping experience. They have also scaled their infrastructure efficiently to accommodate growing demand.

6. **Stripe**: Security and Compliance
- Background: Stripe, a payment processing platform, places a strong emphasis on security and compliance.
- Outcome: Observability has allowed Stripe to proactively detect and respond to security incidents and ensure compliance with industry regulations. Their robust observability practices have helped maintain customer trust in handling sensitive financial data.

7. Airbnb: Improving Incident Response
- Background: Airbnb, a global online marketplace for lodging, relies on observability to maintain service reliability.
- Outcome: By focusing on incident response and learning from post-incident reviews, Airbnb has reduced the impact of incidents and improved system resilience, leading to a more

reliable platform for hosts and guests.

These case studies and success stories showcase the wide-ranging benefits of a culture of observability. From improving system reliability and performance to enhancing security, organisations across various industries have achieved remarkable results by prioritising observability practices. These real-world examples serve as inspiration and practical guidance for organisations looking to embark on their own observability journey.

In summary, you will hopefully now understand that observability is not just a set of tools and practices—it's a cultural shift that can transform organisations. You are equipped with the knowledge and strategies needed to champion observability initiatives within organisations, fostering a culture where observability is embraced, valued, and woven into the fabric of daily operations. Observability becomes a mindset that drives continuous improvement and ensures that systems are reliable, performant, and secure.

Chapter 12

The Future of Observability

In our final Chapter, we embark on a forward-looking journey into the future of observability. While also recapping on some of the foundational concepts we have covered togather. This chapter explores emerging trends, evolving technologies, and the ever-expanding role of observability in an ever-changing technological landscape.

12.1 Observability in the Age of Complexity

The chapter begins by acknowledging the increasing complexity of modern technology stacks, from microservices and serverless architectures to multi-cloud environments. It emphasises how observability will continue to play a crucial role in taming this complexity by providing insight into intricate systems.

Observability in the Age of Complexity

The complexity of our systems and architectures has grown exponentially. From microservices and serverless architectures to multi-cloud environments, the sheer intricacy of modern technology stacks can be overwhelming. This section delves into the concept of observability and how it remains a critical tool in managing and understanding this ever-increasing complexity.

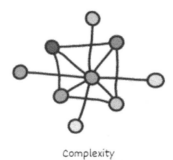

Complexity

1. The Growing Complexity:

Modern technology infrastructures are characterised by their diverse and interconnected components. Microservices, which involve breaking down applications into smaller, independently deployable units, have become commonplace. Serverless computing, where developers focus on writing code rather than managing servers, is on the rise. Additionally, organisations are increasingly adopting multi-cloud strategies to leverage different cloud providers' strengths. While these approaches offer scalability and flexibility, they also introduce new layers of complexity.

2. The Role of Observability:

As a recap, Observability is the ability to gain insights into the inner workings of a system by examining its external outputs. In an age of complexity, observability serves as a beacon of clarity. It involves collecting and analysing data from various sources within a system, enabling engineers to understand its behaviour, identify issues, and make informed decisions.

3. Key Components of Observability:

a. Logging: Traditional logging provides a historical record of events in a system, aiding in post-mortem analysis. However, it may not capture all relevant data and can be challenging to manage in large-scale environments.

b. Metrics: Metrics are quantifiable measurements that offer a snapshot of a system's performance. They provide valuable insights into resource utilisation, response times, and error rates.

c. Tracing: Distributed tracing allows engineers to follow the flow of requests across different microservices, providing a comprehensive view of how a request traverses through a complex system.

4. The Challenges of Observing Complex Systems:

a. Data Overload: In complex environments, the sheer volume of data generated can be overwhelming. It's essential to filter and focus on the most relevant information.

b. Distributed Nature: With microservices and multi-cloud deployments, systems are distributed across various environments, making it challenging to gain a holistic view.

c. Real-Time Analysis: In a world where downtime can be costly, real-time analysis of observability data becomes crucial for proactive issue resolution.

5. Tools and Technologies:

Observability platforms and tools have evolved to address the challenges of complex systems. These tools offer features like log aggregation, distributed tracing, and real-time monitoring, making it easier for teams to gain insights into their systems' behaviour.

6. The Human Element:

While observability tools are indispensable, they are most effective when combined with the expertise of skilled engineers. Human intuition and experience play a vital role in interpreting data and making decisions based on observability insights.

As technology continues to advance and systems become more complex, observability remains a cornerstone of effective system management. It empowers engineers to navigate the intricate web of microservices, serverless architectures, and multi-cloud environments, ensuring the reliability and performance of modern technology stacks. Embracing observability is not just a response to complexity; it is a proactive approach to understanding and taming it.

12.2 AI and Machine Learning in Observability

The integration of artificial intelligence (AI) and machine learning (ML) into observability is a significant trend. The section discusses how these technologies are being applied to automate anomaly detection, predict potential issues, and optimise system performance, making observability more proactive and predictive.

AI and Machine Learning in Observability

Where modern technology stacks involve intricate microservices, serverless architectures, and multi-cloud deployments, the integration of artificial intelligence (AI) and machine learning (ML) into observability is a game-changer. This section explores how AI and ML are revolutionising observability by automating anomaly detection, predicting potential issues, and optimising system performance, ultimately making observability more proactive and predictive.

1. Automating Anomaly Detection:

a. Traditional observability relies on engineers manually setting thresholds and rules to identify anomalies. However, this approach falls short in complex systems, where anomalies may be subtle or hard to anticipate.

b. AI and ML models can analyse vast amounts of data in real time, learning the normal behaviour of a system and automatically detecting anomalies. This dynamic approach is well-suited for complex, ever-changing environments.

2. Predictive Insights:

a. AI-driven observability can predict potential issues before they impact system performance or availability. By analysing historical data and patterns, these systems can provide early warnings and recommendations for preventive action.

b. Predictive insights empower IT teams to proactively address issues, reducing downtime and minimising the impact on users.

3. Root Cause Analysis:

a. AI and ML models can assist in root cause analysis by correlating data from various sources to pinpoint the exact source of an issue. This saves valuable time in troubleshooting and resolving problems.

b. These technologies help identify complex dependencies and interactions in distributed systems, making it easier to trace issues across microservices and cloud providers.

4. System Optimisation:

a. Observability powered by AI and ML can optimise system performance by analysing data and recommending adjustments in real time. For example, it can optimise resource allocation in serverless environments or suggest configuration changes.

b. ML models can help fine-tune parameters, making systems more efficient and cost-effective.

5. Adaptive Learning:

a. AI and ML-driven observability systems continuously adapt to changing environments. They learn from new data and adjust their models to stay effective in dynamic systems.

b. This adaptability is crucial in environments where applications and infrastructure evolve rapidly.

6. Human-Machine Collaboration:

a. AI and ML are most effective when combined with human expertise. Engineers use insights provided by these technologies to make informed decisions and take action.

b. AI and ML can assist in prioritising issues, allowing engineers to focus on critical problems.

The integration of AI and ML into observability represents a significant advancement in managing complex technology stacks. These technologies automate anomaly detection, predict potential issues, optimise system performance, and assist in root cause analysis. By making observability more proactive and predictive, AI and ML empower organisations to maintain the reliability and performance of their systems in the face of increasing complexity. However, it is crucial to strike a balance between automation and human expertise, as both are integral to effective observability in the age of complexity.

12.3 Serverless Observability

As serverless computing gains prominence, observability in serverless environments becomes paramount. You will learn about the unique challenges and opportunities in observing serverless applications and how specialised observability solutions are emerging to address these needs.

Serverless Observability

Serverless computing has gained significant prominence in modern application development due to its scalability, cost-efficiency, and reduced operational overhead. However, as serverless environments become increasingly prevalent, ensuring observability in these architectures becomes paramount. This section explores the unique challenges and opportunities in observing serverless applications and highlights how specialised observability solutions are emerging to address these needs.

1. The Rise of Serverless Computing:

a. Serverless computing abstracts away server management, allowing developers to focus solely on writing code in the form of functions or microservices.

b. Serverless architectures are event-driven, auto-scaling, and inherently distributed, making traditional observability methods less effective.

2. Challenges in Serverless Observability:

a. Cold Starts: Serverless functions experience variable start-up times known as "cold starts," which can impact response times.

Observing and mitigating these delays is crucial.

b. Distributed Nature: Serverless applications are highly distributed and event-driven, making it challenging to trace the flow of requests across functions.

c. Short-Lived Instances: Serverless instances are short-lived, making traditional log-based observability less practical. Valuable data may be lost if not captured in real time.

d. Third-Party Services: Serverless applications often rely on third-party services and APIs, which require observability to ensure their reliability and performance.

3. Specialised Observability Solutions:

a. Real-Time Metrics: Specialised serverless observability solutions offer real-time metrics on function invocations, durations, and resource usage, enabling developers to monitor performance at a granular level.

b. Distributed Tracing: Distributed tracing tools help trace requests as they move across functions and services, providing end-to-end visibility into serverless applications.

c. Error Tracking: These solutions identify errors and exceptions in serverless functions, offering insights into problematic code sections.

d. Cold Start Analysis: Observability platforms provide insights into cold start times, helping developers optimise function performance.

4. Serverless Security: Observability also plays a crucial role in serverless security, helping detect and respond to security incidents and vulnerabilities in real time.

5. Auto-Scaling Insights: Specialised tools provide visibility into auto-scaling behaviour, allowing teams to understand how

serverless applications respond to varying workloads.

6. Cost Optimisation: Observability in serverless can help optimise costs by identifying resource bottlenecks and unnecessary function invocations.

7. Human-Machine Collaboration: While specialised observability tools are powerful, human expertise remains essential. Engineers use insights from observability platforms to make informed decisions and improvements in serverless applications.

As serverless computing continues to gain prominence in the world of cloud-native application development, observability becomes a critical factor in ensuring the reliability, performance, and security of serverless applications. Specialised observability solutions are emerging to address the unique challenges posed by serverless architectures, providing real-time insights into function performance, cold starts, and distributed interactions. By embracing these tools and combining them with human expertise, organisations can effectively observe and manage serverless applications in the evolving landscape of modern computing.

12.4 Edge and IoT Observability

Observability is expanding beyond data centres and into the edge and Internet of Things (IoT) ecosystems. This section explores how observability practices are being adapted to monitor distributed edge devices and IoT deployments, ensuring reliability and security in these critical domains.

Edge and IoT Observability

The rapid growth of edge computing and the proliferation of Internet of Things (IoT) devices have introduced new complexities to the world of observability. This section delves into the evolving practices of observability, which are being adapted to monitor distributed edge devices and IoT deployments. It highlights the significance of observability in ensuring reliability and security in these critical domains.

1. The Expansion of Edge and IoT:

a. Edge computing brings computation closer to data sources, reducing latency and enabling real-time processing. This is critical for applications like autonomous vehicles and industrial automation.

b. IoT encompasses a vast ecosystem of connected devices, from sensors and actuators to smart appliances and wearables, all generating vast amounts of data.

2. Unique Challenges in Edge and IoT Observability:

a. Distributed Nature: Edge and IoT deployments are highly distributed, often spanning multiple locations and devices. Traditional data centre observability models may not apply.

b. Limited Resources: Many edge and IoT devices operate with constrained resources, making it challenging to run resource-intensive monitoring agents.

c. Connectivity Variability: Devices in these ecosystems may have intermittent or low-bandwidth connectivity, requiring observability solutions to adapt.

d. Security Concerns: IoT devices are prime targets for security threats. Observability is essential for detecting and responding to security incidents.

3. Customised Observability Solutions:

a. Lightweight Agents: Observability solutions for edge and IoT often use lightweight agents that consume minimal resources. These agents collect data and forward it to central observability platforms.

b. Edge-Based Processing: Some observability functions, like data preprocessing and anomaly detection, are performed at the edge to reduce latency and minimise the data sent to central servers.

c. Edge Gateways: Edge gateways act as intermediaries between devices and observability platforms, aggregating data and providing local analysis and control.

4. Real-Time Analytics:

a. Real-time analytics are crucial in edge and IoT observability to identify issues immediately and respond to events that require rapid intervention.

b. Machine learning models can analyse data streams at the edge to detect anomalies and trigger alerts or autonomous actions.

5. Security Observability:

a. Security observability, as we have covered in some depth already, is a vital component of edge and IoT deployments. It involves monitoring device behaviour for signs of compromise and responding to security incidents in real time.

b. Threat detection models can be deployed at the edge to identify abnormal patterns and raise alerts.

6. Data Privacy and Compliance:

a. Edge and IoT observability must consider data privacy

regulations and compliance requirements, especially when handling sensitive data from connected devices.

b. Data anonymisation and encryption are essential to protect user privacy and comply with regulations.

7. Human-Machine Collaboration:

a. Human operators play a crucial role in edge and IoT observability by responding to alerts, making decisions, and taking actions based on the insights provided by observability platforms.

b. Automation can assist in routine tasks, but human expertise remains vital.

Observability is extending its reach beyond traditional data centres into the realms of edge computing and the Internet of Things. As distributed edge devices and IoT ecosystems continue to grow in complexity, observability practices are evolving to meet the unique challenges posed by these environments. Customised observability solutions, real-time analytics, security monitoring, and compliance considerations are all critical aspects of ensuring reliability and security in edge and IoT deployments. By embracing observability in these domains, organisations can maintain control, enhance performance, and mitigate security risks in their edge and IoT ecosystems.

12.5 Observability Standards and Open Source Initiatives

The section highlights the importance of observability standards and open-source initiatives. It discusses the role of projects like OpenTelemetry and OpenMetrics in creating a common language and ecosystem for observability, ensuring interoperability and vendor-agnostic observability solutions.

Observability Standards and Open Source Initiatives

In observability, the need for standardisation and open-source initiatives has become increasingly evident. This section underscores the significance of observability standards and explores the role of projects like OpenTelemetry and OpenMetrics in creating a common language and ecosystem for observability. These initiatives play a vital role in ensuring interoperability and promoting vendor-agnostic observability solutions.

1. The Importance of Standards:
a. Observability is a fundamental practice for understanding complex systems, but without common standards, it can become fragmented and challenging to implement consistently across diverse environments.

b. Standards provide a shared language and framework that enable different tools and systems to work together seamlessly.

2. OpenTelemetry: A Common Observability Framework:
a. OpenTelemetry is an open-source project that aims to provide a standardised set of APIs, libraries, agents, and instrumentation to collect observability data, including traces, metrics, and logs.

b. It offers a vendor-agnostic approach, allowing organisations to choose the observability tools and platforms that best fit their needs while maintaining compatibility.

c. OpenTelemetry is a merger of the OpenTracing and OpenCensus projects, unifying the observability ecosystem.

3. Key Components of OpenTelemetry:
a. Instrumentation Libraries: OpenTelemetry provides libraries in various languages to instrument code and collect observability data without significant manual effort.

b. Agents: Agents help collect and forward observability data from applications to centralised observability platforms.

c. Exporters: OpenTelemetry supports a wide range of exporters, allowing data to be sent to various observability backends, including popular choices like Prometheus, Jaeger, and Elasticsearch.

d. Specification: OpenTelemetry defines a common specification for trace and metric data, ensuring interoperability across different implementations.

4. OpenMetrics: A Standard for Metrics:
a. OpenMetrics is an open standard for collecting and exporting metrics, providing a common format for metric data across various systems.

b. It simplifies the process of exposing metrics from applications and services, promoting consistency and ease of integration.

5. Benefits of Standardisation:
a. Interoperability: Observability standards like OpenTelemetry and OpenMetrics enable different observability tools to work together seamlessly, reducing vendor lock-in.

b. Ecosystem Growth: A standardised observability ecosystem encourages the development of a wide range of tools and solutions that can leverage the same data format.

c. Community Collaboration: Open-source initiatives foster collaboration among organisations and individuals, leading to the creation of robust and innovative observability solutions.

6. Challenges and Adoption:
a. While standards like OpenTelemetry and OpenMetrics have gained momentum, widespread adoption takes time, and some organisations may still be transitioning to these standards.

b. The benefits of standardisation will become more apparent as observability practices continue to evolve.

7. Future Outlook:
a. The observability landscape is continually evolving, and standards will play a crucial role in adapting to emerging technologies and practices.

b. Open-source initiatives are expected to grow and expand, fostering a more open and collaborative observability ecosystem.

Observability standards and open-source initiatives like OpenTelemetry and OpenMetrics are instrumental in shaping the future of observability. By providing a common language and framework, these projects promote interoperability, reduce vendor lock-in, and encourage innovation in the observability space. As organisations embrace these standards, they are better equipped to navigate the complexities of modern technology stacks and ensure the reliability and performance of their systems.

12.6 Ethical Considerations in Observability

With increased observability comes the responsibility to address ethical concerns related to data privacy and security. The section explores the ethical considerations surrounding observability and discusses strategies for ensuring that observability practices are implemented responsibly.

Ethical Considerations in Observability

The rapid growth of observability practices, driven by advancements in technology and the need for deep insights into complex systems, brings forth a set of ethical considerations. This section delves into the ethical concerns surrounding observability and explores strategies for ensuring that observability practices are implemented responsibly, particularly in the context of data privacy and security.

1. Data Privacy and Consent:
a. Observability often involves collecting and analysing vast amounts of data, including logs, metrics, traces, and user interactions. This data may contain sensitive or personal information.

b. Ethical observability requires obtaining informed consent from users or stakeholders whose data is being observed. Transparency about data collection, storage, and usage is essential.

c. Data anonymisation and pseudonymisation techniques should be applied to protect individual privacy.

2. Minimising Data Collection:
a. Ethical observability practices involve collecting only the data necessary for monitoring and troubleshooting. Overly intrusive data collection should be avoided.

b. Organisations should regularly review and minimise the types and volume of data collected to reduce potential privacy risks.

3. Data Retention and Deletion:
a. Ethical observability practices include establishing clear data retention policies. Data should not be retained longer than necessary for its intended purpose.

b. Data deletion procedures should be in place to ensure that information is removed when it is no longer needed or when requested by individuals.

4. Security of Observability Data:
a. Observability data is sensitive and valuable. Ethical

considerations demand robust security measures to protect against unauthorised access, breaches, and data theft.

b. Encryption, access controls, and secure storage are essential components of ethical observability.

5. Consent for Third-Party Services:
a. Many observability platforms and tools involve third-party services and cloud providers. Organisations should inform users about the use of these services and obtain consent where necessary.

b. Transparency regarding data sharing and the security practices of third-party providers is critical.

6. Monitoring User Behaviour:
a. When observing user behaviour, ethical considerations come into play. Organisations must clearly communicate the purpose of monitoring and its potential impact on users.

b. It's important to strike a balance between observability for operational purposes and respecting user privacy.

7. Compliance with Regulations:
a. Ethical observability practices include compliance with data protection regulations such as GDPR, CCPA, and HIPAA, depending on the nature of the data being observed.

b. Organisations should have processes in place to respond to data access requests and data breach notifications in accordance with legal requirements.

8. Ethical Oversight and Accountability:
a. Ethical observability practices require oversight at the organisational level. Responsible observability champions within the organisation can ensure that ethical considerations are upheld.

b. Establishing accountability for observability-related ethical decisions is essential, and compliance should be audited regularly.

9. Continuous Ethical Review:
a. As observability practices evolve and technologies change, ethical considerations must be revisited and adapted accordingly.

b. Continuous ethical review ensures that observability practices remain aligned with evolving ethical norms and legal requirements.

Observability practices are invaluable for understanding and maintaining complex systems, but they must be accompanied by ethical considerations that prioritise data privacy and security. Responsible observability involves obtaining informed consent, minimising data collection, securing observability data, and complying with relevant regulations. By integrating ethical considerations into observability strategies, organisations can strike a balance between operational insights and the responsible use of data, ensuring that observability practices align with ethical norms and values.

12.7 The Evolving Role of Observability Practitioners

Observability is not just about tools; it's also about the people who wield them. The section touches on how the role of observability practitioners is evolving, requiring a broader skill set that encompasses data analysis, machine learning, and business acumen.

The Evolving Role of Observability Practitioners

Observability is a critical practice for understanding and managing complex systems, and it's not just about the tools and technologies used. The practitioners who wield these tools play a pivotal role in ensuring the reliability and performance of modern technology stacks. This section explores how the role of observability practitioners is evolving, requiring a broader skill set that encompasses data analysis, machine learning, and business acumen.

1. Traditional Observability Roles:
a. Historically, observability roles were often associated with system administrators, network engineers, and DevOps teams responsible for monitoring infrastructure and applications.

b. These roles focused on setting up and maintaining monitoring tools, responding to alerts, and ensuring system stability.

2. The Modern Observability Landscape:
a. The complexity of modern technology stacks, including microservices, serverless architectures, and multi-cloud environments, has expanded the scope of observability.

b. Observability now encompasses monitoring distributed systems, analysing large volumes of data, and gaining insights into user experience and business impact.

3. The Evolving Skill Set:
a. Observability practitioners are increasingly required to have a broader skill set that includes:

- Data Analysis: Proficiency in analysing large and diverse datasets is crucial for deriving insights from observability data.

- Machine Learning: Understanding machine learning techniques is valuable for predictive analysis and anomaly detection in observability data.

- Business Acumen: Observability practitioners need to connect technical observations with business outcomes, helping organisations make data-driven decisions.

- Cloud Expertise: Familiarity with cloud-native observability tools and practices is essential for monitoring applications deployed in cloud environments.

- Security Awareness: Security observability is a growing concern, requiring observability practitioners to have a strong awareness of security best practices.

- Automation Skills: Automation is becoming increasingly important in observability to handle the growing volume of data and routine tasks.

4. Integrating Observability into DevOps:
a. Observability is no longer a separate function but an integral part of DevOps practices. Observability practitioners collaborate closely with development and operations teams to embed observability from the start.

b. Observability is considered a "shift-right" and "shift-left" practice, meaning it's integrated at every stage of the software development lifecycle.

5. The Role of Observability in Business:
a. Observability is not just a technical concern; it has a direct impact on business outcomes. Observability practitioners must translate technical data into business metrics and ROI calculations.

b. Observability can be a competitive advantage, helping organisations identify opportunities for optimisation and innovation.

6. Tools and Platforms:
a. Observability practitioners leverage a variety of tools and platforms, including observability suites, log management systems, APM (Application Performance Monitoring) tools, and security observability solutions.

b. These tools provide the data needed to monitor, troubleshoot, and optimise systems and applications.

7. Continuous Learning:
a. The field of observability is continuously evolving, with new tools, techniques, and best practices emerging regularly.

b. Observability practitioners must commit to continuous learning to stay current in a rapidly changing landscape.

The role of observability practitioners is evolving in response to the increasing complexity of modern technology stacks. These practitioners require a broader skill set that goes beyond traditional system administration to include data analysis, machine learning, business acumen, and cloud expertise. Observability is not just about monitoring; it's about deriving meaningful insights from data to drive business decisions and ensure the reliability and performance of systems. By embracing this evolving role and staying up-to-date with the latest practices and technologies, observability practitioners can play a pivotal role in the success of their organisations.

12.8 The Continual Journey of Learning

The section concludes by emphasising that observability is an ever-evolving field. It encourages you to stay curious, embrace new technologies, and continue their learning journey, ensuring that they remain at the forefront of observability practices in an ever-changing technological landscape.
The Continual Journey of Learning

Observability is not a static practice; it is a dynamic and ever-evolving field. As technology advances, systems become more complex, and user expectations continue to rise, the importance of observability only grows. In this section's conclusion, we emphasise that observability practitioners are on a continual journey of learning and adaptation.

1. Embracing Curiosity:

a. The landscape of observability is continuously shifting, with new tools, methodologies, and paradigms emerging regularly. Curiosity is a driving force in staying at the forefront of observability.

b. Curious observability practitioners explore new technologies, experiment with novel approaches, and seek to understand the latest developments in the field.

2. Embracing Change:
a. The pace of technological change is relentless, and observability practitioners must be prepared to adapt. What works today may not work tomorrow, and what's cutting-edge now may become standard practice soon.

b. Embracing change means being open to new ideas, approaches, and tools that can enhance observability efforts.

3. Lifelong Learning:
a. Learning in observability is a lifelong endeavour. Whether it's mastering a new monitoring tool, understanding a different programming language, or delving into advanced analytics, the journey of learning never truly ends.

b. Continuous learning is not just about keeping up; it's about staying ahead and driving innovation in observability.

4. Staying Informed:
a. Observability practitioners should actively participate in communities, attend conferences, and engage with thought leaders to stay informed about the latest trends and best practices.

b. Staying informed is not just about individual growth; it also benefits the broader observability community by fostering knowledge-sharing and collaboration.

5. Evolving with Technology:
a. As technology evolves, so should observability practices.

This means being prepared to adopt new tools, methodologies, and approaches that can better address the challenges of ever-changing systems.

b. The ability to adapt and evolve is a hallmark of successful observability practitioners.

6. The Impact of Observability:
a. Observability is not just a technical practice; it has a direct impact on business outcomes. Observability practitioners should strive to connect technical insights with the achievement of business objectives.

b. Demonstrating the value of observability helps secure support and resources for ongoing learning and improvement.

In the dynamic and complex world of observability, the journey of learning is perpetual. It is a journey driven by curiosity, adaptability, and a commitment to staying at the forefront of observability practices. As observability practitioners embrace change, continuously seek knowledge, and apply new skills, they not only enhance their own capabilities but also contribute to the advancement of observability as a discipline. In this ever-evolving technological landscape, the journey of learning is not just a choice; it is an imperative for those who seek to excel in the art and science of observability. I hope through reading through the concepts and foundational elements of Observability you have developed an interest in delving even deeper into the topics I have covered with you.

In summary, in this chapter we have gained insights into the dynamic future of observability. You will now understand how observability is evolving to meet the challenges of increasingly complex and diverse technology ecosystems. Armed with this knowledge, you can adapt to these changes, stay ahead of the curve, and continue to leverage observability as a transformative force in the world of technology. Observability is not just a destination; it's a continual journey of discovery and innovation!

Conclusion

In conclusion "o11y Explained has taken us on a transformative journey through the complex world of observability, shedding light on its fundamental principles, tools, and real-world applications. We embarked on this exploration with the intention of unravelling the mysteries of observability and demystifying the art of gaining deep insights into complex systems.

Throughout our journey, we learned that observability is not merely a buzzword, but a powerful concept that empowers organisations to understand and optimise their systems, driving improvements in performance, reliability, and user experience. We've delved into the key pillars of observability, from logging, metrics, and traces to distributed tracing, anomaly detection, and incident response. With each chapter, we have honed our skills and deepened our understanding of how observability can be applied in diverse contexts.

Moreover, we've encountered multiple definitions and examples illustrating how observability is not just a theoretical concept, but a transformative force that can drive innovation, facilitate collaboration, and unlock new possibilities.

As we wrap up our journey, it is clear that observability is not a destination but an ongoing pursuit. Where complexity is the norm and downtime is costly, the principles and practices of observability are more relevant than ever. With the knowledge gained from this resource, you are now equipped to embark on your own observability journey, armed with the tools and insights needed to make informed decisions, resolve issues efficiently, and continually optimise your systems.

I hope "o11y Explained" has been a valuable resource in your quest to master observability. Remember that the pursuit of observability is a never-ending adventure, and as you apply these principles in your own context, you'll not only improve the reliability of your systems but also contribute to the ever-evolving landscape of observability itself.

Thank you for joining me on this journey, and may your observability endeavours be filled with success and innovation!

Appendices

Glossary of Observability Terms:

1. Observability:

   - Definition: The ability to gain insights into the inner workings of complex systems through data collection and analysis, allowing for proactive monitoring and rapid issue resolution.

2. Monitoring:

   - Definition: The process of continuously collecting and analysing data metrics in real-time or near-real-time to track the performance and health of systems. Monitoring tools help detect anomalies and provide alerts.

3. Tracing:

   - Definition: The practice of tracking the flow of requests or transactions as they traverse through various components of a system, providing visibility into request paths, bottlenecks, and dependencies.

4. Logging:

- Definition: The systematic recording of events, actions, and errors within an application or system. Logs provide detailed context for troubleshooting and debugging.

5. Metrics:

- Definition: Quantitative data points that represent the behaviour or performance of a system, such as CPU usage, memory utilisation, request latency, and error rates.

6. Alerting:

- Definition: The process of setting up predefined thresholds or conditions to trigger notifications or alerts when system metrics or events deviate from expected values.

7. Anomaly Detection:

- Definition: The identification of abnormal or unexpected behaviour in system metrics or events, often using statistical analysis or machine learning algorithms.

8. Dashboard:

- Definition: A graphical user interface that displays key performance metrics and data visualisations in real-time, providing a centralised view of system health.

9. Time Series Data:

- Definition: Data points recorded at regular intervals

over time, often used for tracking changes in system performance and behaviour.

10. Agent:

- Definition: A software component installed on a system or host to collect and transmit data to monitoring and observability tools.

11. Instrumentation:

- Definition: The process of adding code or sensors to applications or services to capture specific data for observability purposes, such as tracing or metrics collection.

12. Distributed Tracing:

- Definition: Tracing the path of a request or transaction as it moves through multiple interconnected services in a distributed system, allowing for end-to-end visibility.

13. Root Cause Analysis:

- Definition: The process of identifying the underlying reason or source of a problem or issue in a system to facilitate its resolution.

14. Incident Response:

- Definition: The organised approach to addressing and mitigating system incidents or outages, often involving a team of responders and predefined procedures.

15. Service Level Indicator (SLI):

- Definition: A specific metric or measurement used to quantify the performance or availability of a service, often used in Service Level Objectives (SLOs) and Service Level Agreements (SLAs).

16. Service Level Objective (SLO):

- Definition: A target level of performance or availability defined for a service, typically based on SLIs, used to measure and maintain the desired service quality.

17. Service Level Agreement (SLA):

- Definition: A formal contract that specifies the agreed-upon performance and availability guarantees between a service provider and a customer.

18. AIOps (Artificial Intelligence for IT Operations):

- Definition: The application of artificial intelligence (AI) and machine learning (ML) techniques to automate and enhance IT operations, including observability and monitoring.

19. Data Retention:

- Definition: The duration for which observability data, such as logs and metrics, is stored and retained for analysis and compliance purposes.

20. Continuous Integration/Continuous Deployment (CI/CD):

- Definition: A set of practices and tools that enable the automated testing, integration, and deployment of code changes, often used to maintain system observability during software updates.

21. Alert Fatigue:

- Definition: The phenomenon where excessive or irrelevant alerts from monitoring systems overwhelm operators or DevOps teams, leading to decreased responsiveness and effectiveness.

22. Log Rotation:

- Definition: The process of archiving or deleting older log files to manage storage space efficiently and ensure that the most recent log data is available for analysis.

23. Downtime:

- Definition: The period during which a system or service is unavailable or not functioning correctly, often measured in terms of hours, minutes, or seconds.

24. Latency:

- Definition: The amount of time it takes for a request

or data packet to travel from the source to the destination, often measured in milliseconds.

25. Throughput:

- Definition: The rate at which a system or component can process or handle incoming requests or data, typically measured in transactions per second (TPS) or bytes per second.

26. Black Box Monitoring:

- Definition: A monitoring approach that treats a system as a "black box" and observes its external behaviour without detailed knowledge of its internal workings.

27. White Box Monitoring:

- Definition: A monitoring approach that provides deep insights into the internal state and performance of a system, often achieved through instrumentation and code-level monitoring.

28. Capacity Planning:

- Definition: The process of forecasting and provisioning resources (such as CPU, memory, storage) to ensure that a system can handle expected workloads without performance degradation.

29. SaaS (Software as a Service):

- Definition: A cloud computing model in which software applications are hosted and provided as services over the internet, eliminating the need for on-premises installation and maintenance.

30. DevOps:

- Definition: A set of practices that emphasise collaboration and communication between development (Dev) and IT operations (Ops) teams to automate and streamline the software delivery and infrastructure management processes.

31. Microservices:

- Definition: An architectural style in which a complex application is decomposed into small, independent services that can be developed, deployed, and scaled independently.

32. Serverless Computing:

- Definition: A cloud computing model in which developers write code as small, single-purpose functions that are executed in response to events, without the need to manage servers or infrastructure.

33. Instrumentation Code:

- Definition: The addition of code elements (such as probes, sensors, or hooks) to an application or service to collect data for observability purposes, such as metrics, tracing, or logging.

34. Cloud-Native:

- Definition: A design and development approach that leverages cloud computing services and principles to build, deploy, and operate applications that are highly scalable, resilient, and adaptable.

35. Containerisation:

- Definition: The practice of packaging and isolating applications and their dependencies into lightweight containers for consistent deployment across different environments.

36. Immutable Infrastructure:

- Definition: An infrastructure management approach in which servers and infrastructure components are never modified once deployed; instead, updates are achieved by replacing the entire component with a new, updated version.

37. Zero Trust Security Model:

- Definition: A security framework that assumes no implicit trust, even within a network boundary, and requires verification of identities, devices, and access privileges for every interaction

38. High Availability (HA):

- Definition: A system design approach that aims to minimise downtime by ensuring that services or components are available and operational even in the presence of hardware failures or other disruptions.

39. Immutable Logs:

- Definition: Log entries that cannot be altered, deleted, or modified once they are written, ensuring the integrity and authenticity of log data for compliance and security purposes.

40. Trace Sampling:

- Definition: The practice of capturing and recording only a subset of distributed traces to reduce the overhead of tracing in high-throughput environments while still gaining valuable insights.

41. Golden Signals:

- Definition: A set of critical metrics that represent the health and performance of a service, typically including latency, error rate, traffic, and saturation (often known as the RED method).

42. Correlation ID:

- Definition: A unique identifier assigned to a request or transaction that is passed through various system components, enabling the correlation of logs, traces, and metrics related to that request.

43. Log Aggregation:

- Definition: The process of collecting log data from multiple sources, centralising it, and storing it in a unified repository for analysis and monitoring.

44. Incident Management:

- Definition: The structured process of detecting, reporting, responding to, and resolving incidents and outages in a systematic and efficient manner.

45. Heatmap:

- Definition: A graphical representation of data in which values are depicted as colours, allowing for the visualisation of patterns and trends in metrics or usage data.

46. Continuous Monitoring:

- Definition: The ongoing process of monitoring systems, applications, and services without interruption, providing real-time insights into their health and performance.

47. Metric Aggregation:

- Definition: The process of combining multiple individual metric data points into summary statistics or aggregated values, such as averages, sums, or percentiles.

48. Proactive Monitoring:

- Definition: A monitoring approach that focuses on identifying and addressing issues before they impact users or cause service disruptions, often by setting up automated alerts and triggers.

49. Post-Mortem Analysis:

- Definition: A systematic examination and documentation of a major incident or outage, with the goal of understanding the root causes, identifying preventive measures, and improving incident response procedures.

50. Resource Utilisation:

- Definition: The measurement and analysis of how system resources, such as CPU, memory, disk space, and network bandwidth, are being used by applications and services.

51. KPI (Key Performance Indicator):

- Definition: A quantifiable metric or data point used to evaluate the success or performance of a system, application, or business process.

52. Tagging:

- Definition: The practice of associating metadata or labels with observability data, such as metrics, logs, or traces, to enable filtering, grouping, and querying based on specific criteria.

53. Log Parsing:

- Definition: The process of extracting structured information from unstructured log data, often using regular expressions or parsing rules, to make logs more accessible and useful.

54. Service Discovery:

- Definition: A mechanism or process that allows services and applications to automatically discover and connect to other services or resources within a network or infrastructure.

55. FaaS (Function as a Service):

- Definition: A serverless computing paradigm in which developers write and deploy small, single-purpose functions that are executed in response to events or triggers, without managing server infrastructure.

56. Data Pipeline:

- Definition: A series of data processing stages or steps that transform, enrich, and transport data from source to destination, often used in log and event processing.

57. Telemetry:

- Definition: The automated collection and transmission of data about the behaviour and performance of systems, applications, or services for monitoring and analysis.

58. Deprecation Notice:

- Definition: An official announcement that a particular feature, component, or API will be phased out or removed in a future software release, typically accompanied by guidance on migration and alternatives.

59. Network Topology:

- Definition: A representation of the physical or logical layout and connections of network devices, such as routers, switches, and servers, to visualise network infrastructure.

60. Service Mesh:

- Definition: A dedicated infrastructure layer for managing communication and interactions between microservices, providing features like load balancing, service discovery, and security.

61. Event Correlation:

- Definition: The process of identifying and analysing patterns and relationships among multiple events or alerts to understand their collective impact and root causes.

62. Cost Optimisation:

- Definition: The practice of managing and reducing the operational costs associated with running applications and services, often by optimising resource utilisation and scaling strategies.

63. Dark Launch:

- Definition: A deployment technique in which new features or code changes are released to production but remain inactive or hidden from users, allowing for testing and validation without disruption.

64. Log Retention Policy:

- Definition: A defined strategy or rule for retaining and archiving log data for a specified period, often based on regulatory requirements, compliance, or operational needs.

65. Observability as Code:

- Definition: The practice of defining and managing observability configurations, settings, and instrumentation using code and version control, enabling automation and reproducibility.

66. Golden Ticket:

- Definition: A long-lived authentication token or credential that provides unauthorised access to systems or services, often used in the context of security incidents.

67. Vulnerability Scanning:

- Definition: The automated process of identifying security vulnerabilities, weaknesses, or misconfigurations in software, infrastructure, or systems.

68. Elasticsearch:

- Definition: An open-source, distributed search and analytics engine used for indexing and searching large volumes of structured and unstructured data, commonly used for log and event data storage.

69. Logstash:

- Definition: An open-source data ingestion and transformation pipeline that collects, processes, and forwards log and event data to various destinations, often used in conjunction with Elasticsearch and Kibana (ELK Stack).

70. Kibana:

- Definition: An open-source data visualisation and exploration tool that provides a user-friendly interface for searching, analysing, and visualising data stored in Elasticsearch, commonly used in log analysis.

71. Resilience Engineering:

- Definition: An engineering discipline that focuses on designing systems and software to withstand and recover from failures and disruptions, emphasising fault tolerance and graceful degradation.

72. Synthetic Monitoring:

- Definition: The practice of simulating user interactions and transactions with a system or application to monitor its performance and availability from an external perspective.

73. Observability Maturity Model:

- Definition: A framework or assessment model that categorises organisations' observability practices into stages or levels of maturity, helping them identify areas for improvement.

74. Security Information and Event Management (SIEM):

- Definition: A comprehensive solution that combines security information management (SIM) and security event management (SEM) to provide real-time analysis of security alerts and events from various sources

.75. Operational Excellence:

- Definition: One of the pillars of the AWS Well-Architected Framework, emphasising the efficient and effective operation of systems and applications, including monitoring and observability practices.

76. OpenTelemetry Collector:

- Definition: A component of the OpenTelemetry project that collects, processes, and exports telemetry data, including traces and metrics, from various sources to observability backends.

77. Sampling Rate:

- Definition: The rate at which data points, such as traces or metrics, are collected and recorded, often expressed as a percentage or fraction of the total data.

78. Mean Time to Detection (MTTD):

- Definition: The average amount of time it takes to detect and identify an issue or incident from the moment it occurs, often used as a key performance indicator for incident response.

79. Mean Time to Resolution (MTTR):

- Definition: The average amount of time it takes to resolve an issue or incident from the moment it is detected, often used as a key performance indicator for incident management.

80. Full-Stack Observability:

- Definition: The practice of monitoring and gaining insights into the entire technology stack of an application or system, including infrastructure, networking, application code, and user experiences.

81. Observability Budget:

- Definition: A predefined limit or threshold for the volume of telemetry data, such as traces, logs, or metrics, that can be collected and retained, often used to manage costs and resource consumption.

82. Observability Pipeline:

- Definition: A series of interconnected tools and processes used to collect, process, store, and visualise observability data, facilitating end-to-end observability practices.

83. High Cardinality:

- Definition: A characteristic of data where there are a large number of unique values or dimensions, often challenging for storage and analysis due to its potential impact on performance and resource usage.

84. Latency Histogram:

- Definition: A statistical distribution of latency measurements that provides insights into the distribution of response times for requests or transactions, often used to identify outliers and performance anomalies.

85. Open Source Observability:

- Definition: The use of open-source software and tools for building and maintaining observability practices, often driven by the community and available for customisation and integration.

86. Observability Data Lake:

- Definition: A centralised and scalable data repository that stores and manages observability data, such as logs, traces, and metrics, for long-term retention and analysis.

87. Observer Effect:

- Definition: A phenomenon in which the act of monitoring or observing a system can influence or impact its behaviour or performance, potentially leading to skewed results or conclusions.

88. Regression Analysis:

- Definition: A statistical technique used to analyse the relationship between variables, often applied to observability data to understand the impact of changes or events on system behaviour.

89. Observability Governance:

- Definition: The establishment of policies, processes, and controls for managing observability practices within an organisation, ensuring consistency, compliance, and best practices.

90. Observability Toolchain:

- Definition: A collection of tools and technologies used to implement and manage observability practices, often including monitoring, tracing, logging, and visualisation tools.

91. Chaos Engineering:

- Definition: A discipline that involves intentionally introducing controlled failures and disruptions into a system to assess its resilience, often used to identify weaknesses and improve system robustness.

92. Service Mesh Observability:

- Definition: The set of practices and tools used to gain insights into the behaviour and performance of microservices within a service mesh, often including metrics, traces, and distributed tracing.

93. Data Privacy Compliance:

- Definition: The adherence to regulations and standards related to the protection of sensitive and personally identifiable information (PII) within observability data, ensuring privacy and legal compliance.

94. Real User Monitoring (RUM):

- Definition: A form of observability that focuses on

monitoring the experiences and interactions of actual users with a system or application, often used for optimising user experiences.

95. Observer Bias:

- Definition: A cognitive bias in which observers' expectations or prior beliefs influence their perception and interpretation of observability data, potentially leading to subjective judgments.

96. Log Aggregation Layer:

- Definition: An intermediary component or system that collects, consolidates, and forwards log data from multiple sources to a centralised log repository or analytics platform.

97. Multi-Cloud Observability:

- Definition: The practice of monitoring and gaining insights into applications and services deployed across multiple cloud providers, enabling visibility into a diverse and distributed ecosystem.

98. Observability Data Sampling:

- Definition: The selective collection of observability data, such as traces or logs, at specific points or intervals to reduce the volume of telemetry data and minimise overhead.

99. Observability Workflows:

- Definition: Defined sequences of actions and tasks performed by teams and tools in response to observability data, often involving incident detection, investigation, and resolution.

100. Observability Governance Framework:

- Definition: A structured approach to establishing policies, procedures, and controls for the effective management and governance of observability practices within an organisation.

This extended glossary contains 100 observability terms and definitions, providing a comprehensive reference for understanding key concepts and terminology in the field of observability.

Observability Tools And Resources:

1. Prometheus:
   - Official Website: https://prometheus.io/
   - GitHub Repository: https://github.com/prometheus/prometheus
   - Prometheus is a widely used open-source monitoring and alerting toolkit designed for reliability and scalability. It excels at collecting metrics from various sources and has a robust query language (PromQL) for analysing them.

2. Grafana:
   - Official Website: https://grafana.com/
   - GitHub Repository: https://github.com/grafana/grafana
   - Grafana is an open-source platform for monitoring and observability that allows you to visualise and analyse metrics and logs through customisable dashboards.

3. Elasticsearch, Logstash, and Kibana (ELK Stack):
   - Official Website: https://www.elastic.co/
   - GitHub Repositories:
     - Elasticsearch: https://github.com/elastic/elasticsearch
     - Logstash: https://github.com/elastic/logstash
     - Kibana: https://github.com/elastic/kibana
   - ELK Stack is a popular open-source solution for centralised logging and log analysis. Elasticsearch stores logs and metrics, Logstash processes them, and Kibana provides a user-friendly interface for searching and visualising the data.

4. Fluentd:
   - Official Website: https://www.fluentd.org/
   - GitHub Repository: https://github.com/fluent/fluentd
   - Fluentd is an open-source data collector designed to unify log data collection and delivery. It can ingest data from various sources and forward it to numerous destinations, making it highly versatile.

5. Jaeger:
   - Official Website: https://www.jaegertracing.io/
   - GitHub Repository: https://github.com/jaegertracing/jaeger
   - Jaeger is an open-source, end-to-end distributed tracing system that helps monitor and troubleshoot microservices-based applications by tracking requests as they flow through different components.

6. OpenTelemetry:
   - Official Website: https://opentelemetry.io/
   - GitHub Repository: https://github.com/open-telemetry/opentelemetry
   - OpenTelemetry is an open-source project that provides a set of APIs, libraries, agents, and instrumentation to provide observability for cloud-native software. It supports tracing, metrics, and more.

7. InfluxDB:
   - Official Website: https://www.influxdata.com/
   - GitHub Repository: https://github.com/influxdata/influxdb
   - InfluxDB is an open-source time series database that is often used for storing and querying metrics and performance data. It integrates well with other tools like Telegraf and Grafana.

8. Zipkin:
   - Official Website: https://zipkin.io/
   - GitHub Repository: https://github.com/openzipkin/zipkin
   - Zipkin is an open-source distributed tracing system that helps trace requests as they travel across various services in a

distributed system.

These open-source observability tools cover a range of use cases, from log aggregation and analysis to metric monitoring and distributed tracing. Depending on your specific requirements and the complexity of your environment, you may choose one or more of these tools to gain insights into your systems.

1. Instana:
- Website: https://www.instana.com/
- Instana is a leading provider of Application Performance Monitoring (APM) and observability solutions. It offers real-time monitoring and automatic tracing of application performance, dependencies, and infrastructure.

2. Datadog:
- Website: https://www.datadog.com/
- Datadog is a cloud-based monitoring and analytics platform that provides comprehensive observability for cloud-scale applications. It offers monitoring of metrics, traces, and logs in one integrated platform.

3. New Relic:
- Website: https://newrelic.com/
- New Relic is an APM and observability platform that helps organisations monitor the performance of their applications and infrastructure. It offers insights into application performance, errors, and infrastructure health.

4. Dynatrace:
- Website: https://www.dynatrace.com/
- Dynatrace is an observability platform that provides AI-driven, full-stack monitoring for cloud-native environments. It offers automatic discovery and tracing of application components.

5. AppDynamics:
  - Website: https://www.appdynamics.com/
  - AppDynamics, a Cisco company, offers APM and observability solutions for monitoring application performance, user experience, and business impact in real-time.

6. Splunk:
  - Website: https://www.splunk.com/
  - Splunk is a data analytics and observability platform that allows organisations to collect and analyse machine data, including logs, metrics, and events, for troubleshooting and insights.

7. Sumo Logic:
  - Website: https://www.sumologic.com/
  - Sumo Logic is a cloud-native, machine data analytics platform that helps organisations collect and analyse logs and metrics for security and operational insights.

8. Nagios:
  - Website: https://www.nagios.org/
  - Nagios is an open-source monitoring and alerting system that provides a flexible framework for monitoring IT infrastructure, including servers, networks, and services.

9. Zabbix:
  - Website: https://www.zabbix.com/
  - Zabbix is an open-source monitoring solution that can monitor various aspects of your IT infrastructure, including servers, networks, applications, and more.

10. SolarWinds:
  - Website: https://www.solarwinds.com/
  - SolarWinds offers a range of IT monitoring and management tools, including network monitoring, application performance management, and log analysis solutions.

These vendors offer a wide range of monitoring and

observability solutions to suit various needs, from application performance monitoring and infrastructure monitoring to log analysis and security monitoring. The choice of vendor will depend on your specific requirements and the scale of your monitoring needs.

People and Quotes

1. Charity Majors
   - Role: Co-founder and CTO of Honeycomb
   - Quote: "Observability is about turning the lights on inside your system so you can understand what it's doing, even when it's misbehaving."

2. Cindy Sridharan
   - Role: Senior Infrastructure Engineer
   - Quote: "Observability is not just about logs, metrics, and traces; it's about the intersection of them all. Observability is an empirical, multidisciplinary approach to gaining insight into the behaviour of complex systems."

3. Jaana Dogan
   - Role: Principal Engineer at AWS
   - Quote: "Observability is a mindset shift from 'hope' and 'luck' to a scientific approach with well-defined methodologies to discover, analyse, and troubleshoot unknown unknowns."

4. Liz Fong-Jones
   - Role: Principal Developer Advocate at Honeycomb
   - Quote: "Observability is a journey, not a destination. It's about understanding how your software behaves in production, not just the idealised model you built in your head."

5. Ben Sigelman
   - Role: CEO and Co-founder of LightStep (now part of ServiceNow)
   - Quote: "Observability is about understanding what your software does in production, and if you don't understand it,

you're flying blind."

6. Daniel "Spoons" Spoonhower
   - Role: CTO and Co-founder of LightStep (now part of ServiceNow)
   - Quote: "Observability is about discovering the unknown unknowns—understanding not just what you expect to happen, but what's actually happening in your system."

7. Christine Yen
   - Role: Co-founder and CEO of Honeycomb
   - Quote: "Observability is the path to understanding and managing complexity in a world where systems are distributed, dynamic, and constantly evolving."

8. Benjamin Hindman
   - Role: Co-founder and Chief Architect at Mesosphere (now part of D2iQ)
   - Quote: "Observability is about building a bridge between what developers understand and what operators need to keep systems running."

9. Mikolaj Pawlikowski
   - Role: Software Engineer at Bloomberg
   - Quote: "Observability is the lighthouse that guides us through the stormy seas of complex distributed systems."

10. Alois Reitbauer
   - Role: Chief Technology Strategist at Dynatrace
   - Quote: "Observability is the compass for navigating the wilderness of modern software landscapes."

11. Austin Parker
   - Role: Principal Developer Advocate at LightStep (now part of ServiceNow)
   - Quote: "Observability is the flashlight that shines light on the darkest corners of your systems, revealing both the planned and the unplanned."

12. Priyanka Sharma
   - Role: General Manager of the Cloud Native Computing Foundation (CNCF)
   - Quote: "Observability is about gaining a deep understanding of your system's behaviour, like reading the pulse of your applications and infrastructure in real time."

13. Dave McAllister
   - Role: Director of Open Source at Splunk
   - Quote: "Observability is not just about monitoring, but about creating a living map of your software, helping you anticipate issues before they become problems."

14. Megan O'Keefe
   - Role: Developer Advocate at Grafana Labs
   - Quote: "Observability is like having a microscope for your software, enabling you to zoom in on any part of your system to see what's happening."

15. Lorin Hochstein
   - Role: Principal Distributed Systems Engineer at Netflix
   - Quote: "Observability is about knowing the truth about your system, even when it doesn't behave the way you expect it to."

16. Christoph Neumüller
   - Role: Senior Software Engineer at Google
   - Quote: "Observability is the art of stitching together the story of your system's behaviour, one event at a time."

17. Yuri Shkuro
   - Role: Software Engineer at Uber (Creator of Jaeger, an open-source distributed tracing system)
   - Quote: "Observability is the practice of listening to your system's whispers, shouts, and cries for help and understanding their meaning."

18. Daniel Salt
- Role: Senior Technical Specialist at IBM, Observability, AIOps

- Quote: "Observability promotes both accountability and transparency, aligning everyone, from developers and operations teams to product managers and executives, around a common understanding of system behaviour."

These experts, along with the previous ones, have made significant contributions to the field of observability, and their insights continue to shape how organisations monitor, diagnose, and optimise complex distributed systems.

Thank you for investing your time and energy into reading. I hope it has been helpful for you.

For diving deeper and exploring further insights, you're warmly invited to visit Danielsalt.com.

If you found this resource helpful in anyway I would be sincerely grateful if you could take a moment to leave a positive review on Amazon. Your reflections not only assist me, but other readers in their selection, also provide invaluable feedback that helps shape and enhance future revisions as I seek to keep this book updated and relevant for all future readers.

www.ingramcontent.com/pod-product-compliance
Lightning Source LLC
La Vergne TN
LVHW051223050326
832903LV00028B/2224